UNLOCK YOUR INNER BUDDHA

UNLOCK YOUR INNER BUDDHA

The Keys to Opening Your Mind to Survive and Thrive

DR. THERESA DEL TUFO

PRECOCITY PRESS

Editor: Brenda Lange
Cover Design: Susan Shankin
Cover Photograph: Joe del Tufo
Book Design and Layout: Susan Shankin
Author Photo: Joe del Tufo
Precocity Press, Los Angeles, CA

ISBN: 979-8-9909460-8-8 (Paperback)
ISBN: 979-8-9909460-9-5 (eBook)

Library of Congress Control Number: 2024926105

First edition printed in the United States of America

DEDICATION

This book is dedicated to my late great brother Sonny (Noel) Izon, who inspired me to write it. He was a brilliant artist and filmmaker, and championed the Filipino cause by inspiring pride and enthusiasm through his award-winning films, such as *An Untold Triumph: America's Filipino Soldiers; One Hundred Years of Filipinos in America;* and his masterpiece, *An Open Door: Jewish Rescue in the Philippines.*

This book is also dedicated to the next generation of Izon men and women, who carry his genetic make-up.

Sonny had left the world indelible
Footprints on the Sands of Time,
which will remain intact for all eternity.

Contents

PART 2
For Communities and the Larger Society

Preface

We are at an existential crossroads in our country. We have a choice to make—soar free of our limited lives and liberate ourselves from forces that impair our abilities to survive and thrive, or choose to succumb to the tyranny of intimidation and self-immolation. Our objective in writing this book is to shine a light on the individual and collective challenges confronting us, listen to voices of others who might offer clarity and hope on a path forward (Eastern beliefs and practices, like Buddhism), inspire us to problem-solve, and take constructive actions. We hope to present to the readers emerging patterns of behavior that could serve as guidelines for action and resolution, or at least start the process of collective reflection, learning, and action.

What do you do when life falls apart? Or when the future of our country is compromised by leaders and decision makers who govern by lying and fear, who are intimidated by the truth, or are inclined to consolidate power in a single individual or group? There appears to be wholesale confusion and normlessness in our country—like the January 6, 2021, insurrection, the climate change moving at a speed faster that scientists anticipated, the wholesale corruption and lack of moral vision among our leaders, and the inability of our leaders to communicate and collaborate to solve crucial and life-changing issues that affect us all. The citizens are not doing any better. Despite the external threat of the continuing pandemic, the war in Ukraine, and Israeli-Hamas conflict, we claw at each other instead of collaborating and supporting to overcome internal and external threats. There's wholesale violence in our cities, more guns than people, racial and gender injustice, rising poverty, and a long list of other chronic and immense problems.

How do we even begin to mitigate these national and universal problems facing us? First, we propose to present these problems to raise awareness, clearly identify what the problems are, and do a laser-focus analysis of some possible approaches to effectively address the problems. We offer a new vision and present fact-based information and knowledge to empower readers to change perspectives and mindsets, and hopefully, behaviors. We borrow tested ideas from Eastern and other non-traditional practices and share knowledge from diverse disciplines (from Biology, Psychology, Sociology, Philosophy, and History), and introduce theories from great thinkers. We hope to challenge conventional ideas to reshape mindsets, cultural norms and values, and national policies. We feel that personal and collective growth happens when we challenge readers to move out of their comfort zones.

We firmly believe in our capacity for goodness and greatness, and in our ability to generate the brilliance and the power that are inherent in all of us—a change in perspective that will allow us to continue this experiment in democracy.

Dr. Theresa del Tufo

INTRODUCTION

The Power of the Mind
The Buddhist Connection

The awakened mind has a diamond-like clarity.
When this clear insight rests in the heart's tender compassion,
both dimensions of liberation are fulfilled.
Jack Kornfield, *The Mind & the Heart*

BUDDHISTS TEACHINGS CENTER on the power of the mind to liberate us from suffering by changing our perceptual thoughts, which at times create looping negative ideas and stories. Deeper than the subconscious mind is another layer of thought that is naturally good, and this subterranean level is what we need to awaken the mind to mitigate our worldly suffering. Pema Khandro (*The Power of Mind in Buddhist Thought,* 2023) states that it is "Deeper than our subconscious mind, our karmic scripts, our social programming and even deeper than the undigested emotions from traumatic events, there is an underlying, self-existent wakefulness, which is good and clear." This, she notes, is our Buddha-nature, an innate goodness that is embedded in all of us. We simply have to be aware of it to access it, and to understand its nature and power to liberate us from suffering.

First and foremost, what is the mind? In the Western world, we think of the mind only as the rational cognitive process emanating from the brain. Dr. George Banez observed in his essay, *Heeding Sage Advice: The Center of the Mind is the Heart,* (unpublished article, 2023) that "Buddhists distinguish the mind from the brain, the part of the body that generates what we modern humans call *consciousness.* In today's daily parlance, *consciousness* is closest to our concept of the mind."

The mind is an empty vessel—it is up to us to fill it with negative or positive thoughts, which might simply be our interpretation of events and realities that might not even correspond with objective realities. This is a process where we have complete control, even when we are unable to change circumstances. We can deploy our minds to react and cope in a positive and affirming way, or react in a negative, reflexive, and fear-based way. Buddhists believe that meditation is the primary path towards liberation by focusing on the joy and happiness of the moment. Notable American humorist, novelist, and travel writer, Mark Twain, said it best, "My life has been filled with terrible misfortunes . . . most of which never happened."

Part 1: For Individuals attempts to influence minds and behavior by including some pearls of wisdom from Eastern philosophical traditions and practices, such as Buddhism and Taoism. The oneness of life is the theme of the first chapter in *The Not-So-Hidden Mystery of Life,* and several other chapters that follow. The concept of oneness teaches us that every aspect of life is the result of the dynamic interaction between two opposing but complementary forces. They do not nullify each other, but hold each force in a state of creative tension to achieve harmony and balance. The states of happiness and unhappiness ebb and flow in our lives; neither state is permanent. Change is the essence of life—the temporal nature of life defines human existence. All opposites that we experience, such as health and sickness; wealth and poverty; love and hate; suffering and joy; and ultimately life and death can be explained by the dominance of one force over the other. Consider the dual nature of life and death—our penultimate human experience. Blanchard *(Law of Duality,* 2013), summed up the concepts of duality and oneness in this revealing observation, "The Law of Duality basically states that everything is on a *continuum* and has a complementary opposite within the whole. To use an adage, there may be two sides of a coin, but there is only one coin. In other words, things that appear as opposites are in fact only two extremes of the same thing."

Another chapter, *The Fulllness of Nothing,* applies Eastern beliefs to inspire us to learn and grow. The concept of *"Ma"* is a Japanese word, which can be roughly translated as "full of nothing." This mindset is predominant in Japanese art, music, and culture. It can also be applied to life's transitions, or the up-and-down cycle of life. During the down cycle, we go through the disruptive feelings of confusion, disorientation, anxiety, and fear. Although it appears to be a dark and dormant period, there is often an invisible growth during this short and sterile interlude. It is a time for reflection, introspection, and growth. The remaining chapters in Part 1 are seamlessly linked by the use of Eastern beliefs and practices to inspire readers to consider a new approach, a shift in paradigm, or simply a fresh and different orientation to life and living.

Part 2: For Communities and the Larger Society introduces new perspectives and learning by providing new information and knowledge to readers. It explores the Buddhist idea of using the power of the mind and heart to transform communities and societies by *opening minds* to new, vibrant, and validated information and knowledge. In the chapter, *A New Power Model,* the author introduces *Character-Driven Leadership* that focuses on leaders' character and competencies. In *Positive Aging: Finding*

Purpose, Passion, and Joy in Old Age, the author strives to change the mind's gravitational center by pointing out older adults' wealth of knowledge and experience, their cognitive reserve, and their ability to use crystallized intelligence to tackle new problems in creative ways. She presents evidence dispelling negative stereotypes about this marginalized group, and shares information on their ability to learn new information at any age (brain plasticity and aging), and to apply knowledge, with vision and creativity, to solve present and future problems (crystallized intelligence).

PART 1

For Individuals

CHAPTER 1

The Not-So-Hidden Mystery of Life

The Duality of Life

THE DUALITY OF LIFE is a basic Buddhist tenet that anyone aspiring to lead a balanced, happy, and harmonious life might need to fully understand and appreciate. Even as a youngster, questions about life's ultimate realities and purpose occupied my inquiring and hungry mind. I was laser-focused on the mystery of birth and death and what lies in between. The dual nature, but oneness, of life offered a revealing pathway in my life's journey. It's much like snapping a key piece of a Rubik's Cube, although not the final one.

It was only in my early seventies that I started to finally grasp the immutable power of this concept. Although I was aware of the polarities of life, its ups and downs, I avoided the coiled energy of the dark and down times, a reaction typical of all humans. Who enjoys suffering, pain, and illness? Only after I have gone through the transformation that comes with unimaginable grief and life-changing suffering did I begin to understand the power of the other side of life. Only now am I starting to perceive the shadow of its enigmatic face by connecting my mind with my heart and my spirit.

What Does Duality and Oneness in Life Mean?

The concept of oneness teaches us that every aspect of life is the result of the interaction between two opposing but complementary forces. They do not nullify each other, but hold each force in a state of creative tension to achieve harmony and balance. It's much like the playground game of seesaw, with a set of conjoined long, narrow boards supported by a single pivot located at the midpoint between both ends. When one end goes up, the other goes down. It's comparable to the dual wings of an eagle that provide balance to this majestic bird so it can fly.

The states of happiness and unhappiness ebb and flow in our lives; neither state is permanent. *Change is the essence of life—the temporal nature of life defines human existence.* All opposites that we experience, such as health and sickness, wealth and poverty, love and hate, suffering and joy, and ultimately life and death can be explained by the dominance of one force over the other. The Chinese philosophers call this the Yin-Yang rhythm of life. It is traditionally associated with Taoism, a Chinese religion and philosophy that advocates for simplicity and effortless action, while focusing on the contemplative aspects of life rather than material desires. The Yin-Yang paradigm represents all the opposing and contradictory aspects of the universe. Yin is typically feminine, passive, and dark, while Yang is masculine, active, and bright. It is an eternal cycle of reversal because every principle has the seeds of its opposite embedded in its essence (del Tufo, *The Fullness of Nothing,* 2015).

Elements of Duality

Opposite but complementary forces: According to Blanchard (*Law of Duality,* 2013), "The Law of Duality basically states that everything is on a *continuum* and has a complementary opposite within the whole. To use an adage, there may be two sides of a coin but there is only one coin. In other words, things that appear as opposites are in fact only two extremes of the same thing." Consider the dual nature of life and death—our ultimate human experience. Scott Trettenero (July 3, 2020) poses these daring questions:

> *What if it is equally as valuable to experience the non-physical world that death gives us, as it is to experience the*

physical world? Maybe we would not fear death as a lot of us do right now. What if we lived our life not being afraid to die, by knowing that this next aspect of existence was just the other side of the same coin?

Viewing life and death from this perspective, as a continuum and part and parcel of the same coin, makes death less fearful for me. It clarifies the concept of duality and its profound influence in every aspect of our daily lives and the ultimate question of existence. This powerful concept and philosophy need to be part of our public education system, which can greatly improve the quality of our lives. It's a powerful antidote to the deepening conflict and divide that's separating our country right now; the increasing violence in our cities; and the fear, anxiety, confusion, and death caused by the COVID-19 pandemic.

- **Refrain from making judgements:** Good or bad? Right or wrong? To better appreciate and understand the concept of duality, we have to refrain from judging opposite perspectives, such as liberal-conservative, male-female, hot-cold, or Democratic-Republican and so on. When we engage in labeling and judging one side as right or wrong, then we lose clarity on the viability of learning from the opposite perspective. The goal is to stay in the middle and learn from the other individual's perspective. In the same way that we don't know everything about death because we have not experienced it, we can't fully understand the other person's point of view and perception of realities. We need to be intentional, adaptive, and keep an open mind to profit from these conflicting realities.

- **Results in the eternal cycle of change and uncertainty:** The Law of Duality results in an eternal cycle of change and transformation. Nothing stays the same. Uncertainty is baked into every fiber of human existence. It's the law of life. I find this simple but profound reality hopeful and positive, especially when things are tough, like right now. We're in a lockdown fight with an invisible virus, we have a defeated and worn-out populace, and a barren wasteland of mind, heart, and spirit. Knowing that this catastrophic event will someday come to an end could give us a measure of hope, solace, and strength to carry on. Even bad times are transitory; only change is permanent.

Ryan Holiday reminds us of the temporal nature of life in the *Daily Stoics* (It's a Phase, May 25, 2022). He states "It's a phase. All of it. Not just with your kids and the tantrums or the teenage rebellion. But also, with whatever the cultural moment is, be it political correctness or aggressive anti-intellectualism." He cautions us to stay grounded and gently wean ourselves from the anxiety caused by this temporary interlude, "When you're stressed, depressed, anxious, angry, losing hope, you must remind yourself of this too. All of it is a phase." Yes, nothing lasts forever.

- **Seize the moment but be strategic about the future:** On a practical and realistic level, how can you be happy by focusing on the Now? The present moment is the only reality you have. The past is a memory trace and the future is an imagined Now that does not exist. Why worry about a past and a future that you do not have? You can shape this present moment to be a happy interlude and experience it with every fiber of your being. For example, I am sitting on my porch, relishing the refreshing, bright spring sun and smelling the scent of freshly cut grass and the hint of Jasmine in the air. I can cut this happy interlude short by focusing on my worries and fears, or I can continue to enjoy the present moment and savor the gift of life. How you feel at this present moment is up to you—your choice. Is it going to be high-octane happiness or toxic negativity; fear and anxiety or peace and contentment? I certainly don't mean that you should stop taking stock of the problems in your life and curtail your efforts to address and resolve them. You only need to balance the demands of living with your search for self. Constantly complaining about your lot in life indicates that you're transferring the blame or the responsibility to resolve the issue. You must do three things: one, take steps to resolve the problem; two, stop complaining if the problem is beyond your span of control; finally, accept responsibility for the problem if you're part of the cause (del Tufo, *The Fullness of Nothing,* 2015).

How to Benefit from the Law of Duality

- **Understand and accept life's contradictions:** Much like the proverbial duality of life, we find that life is replete with contradictions. There is perfection in imperfection, beauty can coexist with a flawed character, there are brutal dictators capable of deep and transforming love. Despite the unfathomable despair and visceral pain palpable in the faces of the besieged Ukrainians, there is a sea of hopeful, courageous, and resilient faces standing up to the Russian aggressors. Life is complex and multi-faceted. We can survive and thrive if we accept differences and incompatible circumstances that are not within our span of control, if we continue to practice resilience, and do our level best to address those problems that we can control. I can say without hesitation that my ability to flourish in this country is due in large measure to my resilience and ability to adapt to difficult circumstances and changing cultural norms. As a child of war, a young widow, and a first-generation immigrant, resilience and hard work allowed me to succeed and find happiness in this new frontier. The martial artist and well-known actor, Bruce Lee counsels us to be like water, "Be shapeless. Be formless. Like water. When you pour water in a glass, it becomes the glass. When you pour water into a cup, it becomes the cup. When you pour water into a tea pot, it becomes the tea pot. Water can flow, or water can crash. Be water my friend."

- Find balance and harmony: Beauty, wealth, intelligence, fame, and their opposites can be the likely source of happiness or unhappiness depending on how we approach life. The law of duality admonishes us to stay at the middle to achieve balance and satisfaction. For example, my husband's untimely death caused my sons and me great unhappiness, anxiety, and fear. It also taught us to be stronger, more self-reliant, and resilient. We survived and continue to thrive because we have strong connections—a village of family, friends, and neighbors supporting us, a belief in the goodness of life, and an all-consuming purpose to continue to live the good life for ourselves and for others. We were challenged by the pain and confusion of death, but we didn't abandon our zest for life. As Nigerian poet Ijeoma Umebinyuo warns us in her poem *Three Routes to Healing* (*Questions for Ada,* 2021):

  You must let the pain visit you,
  You must allow it to teach you,
  You must not allow it to overstay.

The tragedies in life make us stronger and battle-ready for the next struggle, and allow us to have a deeper insight and appreciation of the good times in life. Reverend Martin Luther King gave us an insightful hint of what's possible in a complex and sometimes conflicting world of dualities when he concluded, "But life at its best is a creative synthesis. It is bringing together of opposites into fruitful harmony." *(A Tough Mind and a Tender Heart)*

- The power of choice: The human will is a gift from the Divine, which we can deploy when faced with two opposing and sometimes contradictory choices. Having a pandemic at this moment in time is beyond our span of control—we had no choice in its unrelenting spread with its deadly consequences. We can only control our own reaction to this event. We can minimize its spread by getting vaccinated, wearing a mask, getting tested, and staying home if we test positive to the virus. It's also incumbent on us to get information from scientists and physicians and avoid questionable sources of fake news and misinformation.

A good friend of mine felt devastated when her only son refused to be vaccinated or wear a mask. He appears to have been influenced by the right-wing media and his friends, co-workers and neighbors, who got their information from social media and fake news outlets. She insisted on presenting evidence to her son to convince him to change his mind, but his mind was closed and he told her so. She insisted on the righteousness of her stand and pushed her feeble approach to force him to change behavior. They ended up in a shouting match, which made matters worse. Now the lines of communication are closed, at least for a period of time, and the relationship has been irreparably damaged. Any influence she could have had is now off the table, as he continues to take nourishment from the swamp of misinformation that surrounds him. We have to be strategic in our choices, and consider that our grown children have their own opinions and perceptions. We have no control over their minds or behaviors. We only have control over our own actions and mindset, and have to reflect, adjust, and adapt our responses to achieve harmony and balance. Let go of things you cannot change, instead focus on areas of priorities that you are able to improve and transform.

CHAPTER 2

Fear and the Courage to Be

WHAT HAPPENED to that bold, spontaneous, vibrant risktaker of my youth? She appears to be suspended in a confusing metaverse of fear, anxiety, and confusion. There are flickers of hope; avoidance is not complete. She is taking the first step to pull herself out of the black hole—a semi-controlled anxiety phase, with a glimmer of hope, spiced with a growing determination to minimize its grip, and live with the omnipresent fear.

In my youth, I experienced the freedom and excitement of living in a new frontier, the emerging new suburb named Quezon City. My playmates and I had a vast playground of uninhabited land, green grass, peppered with the remnants of World War II. We used to play inside the rusty and dilapidated tanks left by the American GIs during the war. We played pretend soldiers, pretend doctors, and pretend musketeers. We ran wild, climbed trees, and rolled dried leaves into make-believe cigarettes. We were children of war, but the emotional scars of that dark and hellacious period didn't seem to permanently damage us.

After graduating from college, I volunteered to go to the war-torn country of Laos, which in the 1960s was overtaken by communist insurgents. But my parents refused to let me go; instead, I ended up at the Ateneo Graduate School that opened its doors to women for the first time. It was a Jesuit University that previously was open only to men. It was at this university where I met my future husband, who was teaching at the graduate school at that time. At age 23, I convinced my father to send me to America to continue my graduate work. With my future husband in tow, I left the country of my birth, and stopped by San Francisco and Philadelphia before landing in Dover, Delaware. I grew up in Manila and Quezon City, both of which were cosmopolitan cities, cultural hubs in the mid-1960s, and landed in the sleepy little town of Dover. What a culture shock! There were some hilarious misadventures during this dark and strange transition period, but I eventually enjoyed the simple pleasures and freedom in this capital city of the state of Delaware.

I settled into the peace and routine of ordinary life, gave birth to two good sons, and returned to work when they got older. The peace and tranquility of my married life was shattered when my young husband died of cancer, barely a year after diagnosis. It was at this time that I first experienced the numbing fear and trembling, which before that moment was simply a muscle memory from when I was but a toddler during the Japanese occupation of the Philippines. This tragedy reminded me of the trauma I experienced as a child of war. It brought back painful memories of the attacks and bombing—heartbreaking and iconic snapshots visually unfolding in my mind's eye. I saw my blank face, etched with wild fear and confusion, much like the Syrian boy, Omran Daqneesh, and the besieged Ukrainian children, running for their lives. My husband's death made me feel defeated and beaten down by fate, but buoyed by the conviction that maybe, the furies will stay away from me because they have already robbed me of my most treasured "possession." With defiance and determination, I vowed to live a long and productive life and raise my sons to be happy and well-adjusted young men.

Life resumed its normal rhythm again, I flourished in my jobs, got promotions, and travelled to close to three dozen foreign countries in Europe, Asia, and the Caribbean, mostly by myself. In 1997, I worked in Japan as an exchange administrator, where I collaborated with the International Section of the Miyagi Prefecture. I decided to retire early and do consulting to be able to use my untapped skills and abilities. It was at this time that the unfamiliar face of fear surfaced again, with its gripping and fierce embrace that left me scared and witless. After a regular check up with my gynecologist, he found suspicious growths in my uterus and ovaries, which meant that I had to have a hysterectomy. I went through it successfully, and prognosis was good—no malignancies. However, this baseline fear never left me from that point on. Although I was not always in utter panic, my health concerns and safety and health of my sons kept me in constant communication with fear, anxiety, and other unwelcome guests. I have tried to negotiate an armistice with fear and anxiety, but periodic visitations became part of the routine. Although not unrelenting, fear became part of my behavioral repertoire as I moved into the dawning of the new century.

The Anatomy of Fear

Good fear: Fear is omnipresent in our society and is a fundamental element of the human condition. It is part of the essence of life—much like suffering, pain, and death, and their opposites—joy, health, and life. It is part of the dual nature of life, the yin-yang rhythm of life. Fear can be a useful and protective emotion. As bestselling author Harriet Lerner (2004) reminds us "Throughout the evolutionary history, anxiety and fear have helped every species to be wary and to survive. Fear can signal us to act, or, alternatively, to resist the impulse to act." The other day I was doing my walking meditation and spotted a wild-looking, lethargic red fox from afar, with its tongue sticking out dripping with sticky saliva. My gut feeling told me, in no uncertain terms, to get out of there and head home pronto because that wild beast didn't look normal. The next day I heard from a neighbor that the local wild life agency captured it and found that the animal was infected with rabies.

Chronic and dysfunctional fear: In the close to twenty years that fear has emerged in my life, it has progressively taken over my life and squeezed the joy juice out of everyday living. My overactive amygdala is always on call on every little worry or concern about my sons and my health. This seismic shift in perception and reaction to fear happened exponentially during the current COVID-19 pandemic, when I have more discretionary time and my mind is not as engaged in creative pursuits. It is when my mind is not fully engaged that fear, anxiety, and worry hijack my ability to think clearly and to problem-solve.

What are the characteristics of the negative aspects of fear? First, it is chronic, persistent, and it affects your daily living. Every day is a new worry about your blood pressure or your kids getting COVID, or any other life event that you can't even control. You might worry about the stormy weather, the starving children in India, or the war in the Ukraine. It's serial worrying, every day, with no end in sight. It can morph into a generalized anxiety disorder. Secondly, it's *difficult to resolve* because the overall anxiety and fear robs you of the ability to think clearly and to problem-solve effectively. This is when it has evolved into a disorder, and you have to consult a trained therapist.

Practical solutions to alleviate fear and anxiety: I try to be ruthlessly strategic and focused in alleviating my fear and anxiety, but I realize the enduring power of fear in my life. I know it will resume its periodic visitations, but I am better prepared to handle it after working with a gifted professional and working on my own to deploy some tested practical solutions that have helped me in the past. I am committed to finding health, balance, and happiness in my life. Below is a list of some of the practical tips and antidotes to minimizing the effects of fear and anxiety in my life:

- **Perspective and positive thinking:** It turns out that my fear of death is the root cause of many of my anxieties and fears. I try to embrace this stark reality, because I definitely have no other choice. I find that when I embrace and accept pain, suffering, and death as realities—as constants in life—I am better able to take the first step in opening the door to living a more peaceful, joyful, and free life. It's my ticket to freedom when I summon the bold and creative me! This awakening, an enlightenment of sorts, has given me a new lease on life. Instead of looking at the unfairness and imperfections of life, I now am beginning to appreciate life as a true gift from the universe.

- Power of pretending: When things fall apart, and an individual is confronted with the pain and suffering of say, a chronic and terminal illness, pretending to experience a positive emotion can prove therapeutic. Author Harriet Lerner (2004) notes how one of her clients named Rhoda learned how to harness "the power of pretending and the benefit of distracting herself from fear and pain," as an effective coping technique. Rhoda found out that when she smiled and acted as if she were happy, even when she felt miserable, made her feel better and "lifted her spirits and that pretending to feel joy or courage evoke her capacity for it." As poet Aldo Kraas points out "We are all actors on the stage of life."

- Creative coping: I enjoy exercising like walking fast on a treadmill or enjoying a calming walk in my deserted neighborhood. I also try to feed my soul and still the chatter in my brain by practicing meditation. I combine my two passions and do my walking meditation on my treadmill, especially when the weather is freezing, stormy, or it's too warm outside. I tend to worry too much, especially now that I am partially retired. Dr. Robert L. Leahy suggests experimenting with the following steps to minimize worrying and fear (del Tufo, *The Fullness of Nothing*, 2015):

1. Make a list of your worries: Identify what you're worried about.

2. Analyze the list: Is worrying about the problem productive or unproductive? Is there something you can do to resolve the problem, or is it beyond your control? Is it your problem or does someone else own it?

3. Embrace uncertainty: Problems, uncertainties, and misfortunes are part of the normal rhythm of life. There are times when we have to accept realities that we are unable to influence and change.

4. Bore yourself calm: Say your feared thought again and again until you're tired of hearing it. After hearing it repeatedly, it will lose its hold on you.

5. Make yourself uncomfortable: Face your fears; do not avoid them. If you're afraid of public speaking, practice the skill required by actually doing what you're afraid of until the fear subsides and it powers down to a relaxing relief. Embrace the fear, breathe it in. Let the cleansing energy of your breath transform the fear into an exhilarating feeling of liberation.

6. Stop the clock: According to Dr. Leahy, worried people have an almost uncontrollable sense of urgency. He noted that we need to weigh the advantages and disadvantages

of demanding such urgency and to try to simply observe what's happening at the moment. Focus on the now instead; it's all you have.

7. **Remember that it's never as bad as you think:** Anticipating what could happen is always way worse than actual reality. I always project the worst-case scenario whenever I am confronted with any health issues. My fertile mind spins this tangled web of what-ifs that invariably ends with me suffering from a deadly disease.

Wayne Muller (*Legacy of the Heart,* 2013) cautions us that "In the vain attempt to insulate ourselves from everything that may bring us harm, we sometimes insulate ourselves from life itself." Even when fear appears to lie dormant, it will inevitably show its enigmatic face at some point in our lives. How do we then live with omnipresent fear that peppers our lives? Do we cower in submission or learn how to face it with courage and action?

Lerner states that "Fear is not the problem . . . If you pay attention, you may find that it isn't fear that stops you from doing the brave and true thing in your daily life. Rather, the problem is avoidance." When I feel fear and anxiety crippling me from taking my blood pressure reading, I have a choice—either to relax and take the readings promptly or avoid it altogether and postpone it for a later day, when I am more comfortable doing it. Short-term, I feel more relaxed and can wipe away my worry, but in the long term, I am allowing my fear to morph into a stronger, bolder, and more dominant barrier. I need to cut my losses by facing my fear and deny it of the oxygen that allows it to live and flourish.

Avoidance is the harbinger of greater fear, while courage and bold action diminish its strength and staying power.

CHAPTER 3

The Fullness of Nothing

The concept of "Ma" is a Japanese word, which can be roughly translated as "full of nothing." This mindset is predominant in Japanese art, music, and culture. In music, it is the pause—the silence between musical notes that gives it substance and depth. In Japanese conversation, there is that short silence that allows both the speaker and the receiver to reflect on what was said, fully understand it, and then frame an appropriate response. The only equivalent of the concept of "Ma" in English is the word "empty."

It can also be applied to life's transitions, or the up-and-down cycle of life. During the down cycle, we go through the disruptive feelings of confusion, disorientation, anxiety, and fear. It's much like the uncertainty and fear that we're experiencing right now with the coronavirus pandemic. Author William Bridges (1980) identified this descent as the "neutral zone." This transition phase can be a productive interlude if we think of it as "full of nothing," instead of plain "empty." Dr. Bridges pointed out that ". . . this seemingly unproductive time-out . . . is really an important time for reorientation." Although it appears to be a dark and dormant period, there is often an invisible growth during this short and sterile interlude. It is a time for reflection, introspection, and growth. It's much like the darkness and lack of activity during the dead of winter that blossom into the hope and promise of a bright and vibrant spring day.

I experienced this dark, gaping hole when my husband died. At first, I resisted living in this temporary "neutral zone" that's enveloped by darkness, fear, and anxiety. I tried to convince myself that quick action, jumping back into the fray, and some random activity should propel me to snap out of this spiraling vortex. It didn't work! There were NO shortcuts! I had to give myself time to *simply be*—be miserable, cry my heart out, sleep ten hours a day, or talk to someone if I feel like it. But there's no escaping this dark and dreadful place. I simply had to live through these rotten times. To snap out of this darkness, I first had to accept and experience it. I had to breathe in the fear, the gnawing grief, or the benign anger, or whatever emotion I was feeling at the time. Embracing the raw emotions, breathing them in, stripped away their power. There was no escaping the process. Having survived this period, a respite of sorts, gave me a clearer vision of what I needed to do to survive. Looking back, I can say with conviction that I wouldn't be the person I am today, if I didn't take a respite from ordinary life, plowed through the neutral zone, and embraced the empowering "fullness of nothing."

The take-away here is to embrace the "fullness of nothing" and use this dormant period to reach out and lift someone, take a deep dive into your inner selves and try to search for meaning and purpose. Embrace the fear and accept the darkness that will eventually vanish. Secondly, you might need to adjust your attitudes, and attempt to see the opportunity side of this event rather than the threat to your way of life. Maybe, you might get a job that would make you happier, or have a deeper relationship with a friend or a family member, or realize how really good your life is. Yes, you're stuck at home, but you have ample food, a comfortable house, and now, the time to spend with the people you love. Now is the time to draw up a plan of action. You have this wonderful discretionary time at your disposal. What are you going to do to survive and thrive? You've always wanted to start an exercise regimen to lose weight, go for a walk in the woods, learn to dance, or do yoga. Maybe, you've always wanted to write a novel or learn how to write a poem. For those interested in self growth, you have the gift of time to meditate and reflect on your purpose and your passion. The "Stillness" that best-selling author Ryan Holiday (2019) glorifies is now accessible to you. The author notes that "Stillness is the ability to slow things down. To clarify your thinking. To center your soul. To direct your efforts. To be steady while the world spins." Perfect timing! This is your golden opportunity to be ruthlessly strategic about the direction of your life.

Finally, remember, nothing stays the same—even bad times disappear. Everything in life is temporary! Think about it—the source of your unhappiness and fear can be the source of your newfound peace, meaning, and purpose. This could be your chance to morph into a better version of you! As Americans, we have to ask ourselves difficult questions of character, identity, and legacy. Is this who we are as a nation? Divided, separating at the seams, no one truly listening to one another. We don't trust our leaders and appear to have fragile faith and belief in our democracy. Is this how we would like to shape and remember this experience? Is this our generation's legacy? It doesn't have to be. We all have the power of intentional choice! It's all up to us. Let's take the first step.

CHAPTER 4

Broken Bodies, Broken Minds

Out of suffering have emerged the strongest souls; the most massive characters are seared with scars.
Kahlil Gibran

DAMAGED. BROKEN. TRAUMATIZED. The whole world has been damaged by the COVID-19 pandemic that started in 2020. Our lives are still compromised by the ever-present fear, suffering, and death posed by this rude and unexpected guest. In this country, no one age group has been more affected than older Americans. They are the most at risk of dying from COVID-19, which is validated by the most recent data reported by the Associated Press. More than 700,000 of the one million deaths in this country (as of May 12, 2022) are in the 65 years and older age cohort, which is disproportionate to their population. Seniors have been advised during this pandemic to stay home and avoid large gatherings, which has caused a heavy toll on their mental health, which in turn affects their physical health. This lack of human contact and isolation has resulted in seniors experiencing greater anxiety, depression, and loneliness. According to a study conducted by the University of California, San Francisco (UCSF), the feeling of isolation and lack of connection are predictors of serious health problems, even death. The study notes that loneliness increases the likelihood of mortality by 26 percent, comparable to the damage caused by smoking fifteen cigarettes a day. In addition, lonely individuals have a 64 percent increased rate of developing clinical dementia.

Seniors also experience a whole host of chronic illnesses, such as heart disease, stroke, diabetes, COPD, and other chronic diseases that have a profound impact on the quality of their lives. Their ability to cope is further challenged by the way our society treats and devalues older people. We have a capitalistic society where individuals' worth is inextricably tied to their earning power, which is greatly diminished as they get older.

The loneliness epidemic, which is one of the unintended side effects of staying home in lockdown to prevent the spread of infection, has hit this population in significant ways. I see it in my older friends' blank gaze, in their listless eyes, in their hunched silhouette, defeated gait, and in their silence. They feel beaten down. Hopeless. True, they have the cumulative wisdom, strength, and resilience borne out of the many sufferings and traumas in their lives, but they are not superhuman. They are worn out; beaten down to a pulp. And then some. The mythical resilience and courage to move on are gone. There's not even any attempt to try to "put on their strong hearts." What author Ryan Holiday *(No One is Unbreakable,* 2022) calls "an inner citadel, a fortress of power and resilience that prepares you for the difficulties of the world." Its time has passed—it has been used and abused many times. It's now in a state of obsolescence.

Broken bodies; broken minds. And maybe, broken hearts. Too weak and too exhausted, and beaten down by life to fight back. Death is an easy exit. No more struggles; no need to worry about being a burden. It's a clean break. This is a sentiment that I hear, time and again, voiced by my friends and acquaintances in this at-risk age cohort.

One friend noted that the predicament she is experiencing right now is much like being swallowed by the black hole of our universe, where the gravitational pull is so strong that every glimmer of light is extinguished by the black hole's energy. She recalls how almost every other day, she sees a parade of bodies being wheeled out of her nursing home facility. She calmly recites the stark reality that they're all lined up to take a one-way ride to a destination where there's no way back.

Whatever happened to our mission of taking care of our elderly, the most vulnerable among us—our mothers, fathers, grandparents who took care of us? We talk about "niceties" like recognizing how older adults can play a vital role in our communities and deploying their experience, knowledge, and wisdom. Yes, in some strong communities, I see this model happening, where older citizens remain involved and are integrated into the life of the entire community. During tough times like now, we have to remember to support and care for our older citizens. There are many practical ways that we can alleviate the loneliness and trauma facing our older relatives and neighbors. Engage them in holiday celebrations and other special occasions. They can participate in a video chat or a small gathering. Sons and daughters can connect weekly through email, text, and telephone conversations. Better yet, get vaccinated and wear a mask so you can check on and connect with your elderly mom, dad, and older relatives. Neighbors can check on their elderly neighbors and offer them assistance in tasks they're unable to do, like wheeling their garbage bins to the curb, cutting grass, or going to the groceries for basic items that they need. There are a million and one things to do for our seniors, as long as we care and are willing to help and serve.

Whenever I feel trapped and confused in what feels like a swirling miasma of suffering and pain, I call on an imaginary grandmother. Her name is Lola, and she resurrects before me to share her strength and legendary wisdom. I sit comfortably on her lap, as she engages my hungry heart with stunning narratives of her life experiences. She invariably would end up with a message, not at all didactic or sermonic, but magical and fun. She just has this knack of making learning fun!

Last week, I dropped my ceramic noodle bowl and it broke into several large pieces. Instead of discarding it, I remembered what Lola told me about how she fixed her broken cup by joining the loose pieces with a golden thread of lacquer. She pointed out that she learned this practice when she worked in Japan. In one of our encounters, she told me about this art form called *Kintsugi,* which literally means golden joinery. During my sensible hours, I did some additional research and uncovered interesting facts about this elusive Eastern tradition. Practitioners use gold or silver dust, resin, or lacquer and "glue" the pieces together, with minimal overlap or open space. In philosophy, it celebrates the history of the broken object, rather than hiding it. It embraces its imperfection and designs a new and better version of the broken pieces by putting them back together again, much like people. People are adaptive, resilient and strong, even in the face of unimaginable suffering and pain. They do live and survive—many times, stronger and more courageous than before. *Kintsugi* is a powerful and inspiring metaphor of the totality of human experience. Suffering, illness, and pain are part of the fundamental essence of life, which we need to understand and appreciate. They are a segment of the eternal and predictable cycle of life. Let's allow bad times to help us learn and grow. Allow challenging times to toughen and to transform us and our lives. Its temporary dominance will soon come to its natural end, as we await the coming of a healthier and happier tomorrow.

In the fullness of time, most of us will find the courage to face all the challenges posed by this uninvited pandemic. *Gam zeh ya'avor.* This too shall pass. Live the rest of your brief but spectacular life with an open mind and a courageous heart. Be curious. Be open. Be the best version of you!

CHAPTER 5

How Does It Feel to Be 80?

An AHA Moment

How does it feel to be 80? I whispered to myself that "It's really no different from when I was 40." I am still searching, learning, and hopefully growing. Although, when I glanced at my reflection, I saw this old me, and I screamed in disbelief, then quietly murmured, certainly that cannot be me!

Last weekend, my son and his wife hosted a celebration of my 80th birthday by inviting family and friends, some of whom came all the way from California, New York, Pennsylvania, and

New Jersey. It was an afternoon replete with joy, love, fun, and magic. The healing energy of collective love and joy radiated through every cell of my body so that I almost felt intoxicated with life. Is this how it feels to live in the moment and experience the joy of being alive? The nerve endings in my hands and feet sizzled, much like the sensation I experience whenever I am sipping a glass of red wine. With vivid awareness, I savor it as it slowly rolls down my throat. I savor its swoony and heady charm. I told myself to burn this beautiful memory into my conscious brain.

Much like watching a happy event on film, the happy segment flickered and was replaced by instant fear and apprehension. A loved one had a freak accident—she experienced vertigo, turned around quickly, fell on the floor, and hit her head and thighs. She was in severe pain as she was wheeled out on a stretcher and taken to the nearest hospital in Wilmington, Delaware.

Duality of Life: Balance between Two Competing Forces

The Buddhists teach us about the duality of life—that is every aspect of life is created from a balanced interplay between two seemingly opposite and competing forces. They do not cancel each other out because they are complementary and are part and parcel of the same state, quality, or attribute. For example, dark would not exist without light; there is no death without life; or happiness without pain. This duality is also influenced by the up and down rhythm of life. Today, you're happy and fulfilled, next week, you're miserable, feeling dissatisfied, and beaten down by life. Wait another couple of weeks, and you're on the upswing of the tide of life again. The pendulum of life swings back and forth, much like the steady beat of a metronome.

Pleasure and Pain Can Coexist

As I get older, it seems that the pace of change from one opposite state to another, say from a contented and happy state to a miserable and painful phase, is more frequent and the contrast feels more extreme. Last Saturday, I experienced the boundless joy and exhilaration of family love; strong, loving connections with lifelong friends; and the simmering positive energy generated by the crowd. The next moment, there was all-consuming fear and trembling at the sight of a loved one—suffering and in excruciating pain from an unexpected event. It turned out that the fall resulted in fractures in her brittle bones. From this breathtaking blending of joy and pain in almost a single, infinite moment, I learned that these two seemingly opposite emotions can coexist in an elegant and singular moment in time. What an accidental discovery! This new, exotic approach can be my creative way of surviving and thriving the final passage of my life. Maybe, this cool strategy can help me tame the wall of old age, decay, and death by focusing on moments of joy and positive energy, while holding the negative side in a state of suspension and subconscious acknowledgement. Yes, I am aware of the miserable side of life, I embrace and acknowledge it, but I stop it from taking over my life by not focusing on it. I compare it to the reaction and eventual life that I chose to lead after my husband's death. Once I acknowledged and embraced the grief, darkness, and pain of losing the love of my life, I was able to follow a path that led me to a happy, fulfilled, and satisfying life. I discovered who I am, what I am capable of, and how I can shape a life tailor-made for me.

Flying a Plane While Building It: Planning for Old Age

My son and I planned a couple of months ago to visit a facility for older adults near his home. This arrangement could allow us to spend more time together, and allay his concerns about my safety and health. It was a beautiful and immaculately clean facility; the staff was friendly and courteous; the residents appeared to be happy and well-cared for; and the place was up to standards in terms of common facility measures. We took a deeper dive and proceeded to check out the various types of accommodations available, and the facility staff showed us the various choices in room size. The one-bedroom that I feel I can reasonably afford looks pretty and welcoming, but the size just bothered me. For 57 years, I have lived in a five-bedroom house, with close to 3,000 square feet of livable space. My instinctive reaction was one of fear, doubt, and discomfort. I felt like I have to surgically alter my freedom and expansive life to survive in this cramped space. It is much like stuffing all my life's possessions in my pocketbook, and recreating my identity out of these vital few mementoes of things past. How can I flourish in this hole in a wall and live a morsel of my rich and full life?

I attempted to start the process of planning for my retirement home quite a while back in my seventies. Planning for old age is not an exciting endeavor; it is marbled with apprehension, distaste, and fear. Now planning for an exciting trip, an energizing adventure, is fun and motivating, but planning for old age is unfamiliar and frightening. Intention and planning resulted in timid action. Besides, my eighties just came unannounced, much like an uninvited guest. Now, I am creating a life plan, while I am living it. It is much like flying a plane while I am building it. It is both exciting and terrifying.

Muscle Memory: It Is Like Riding a Bike

I have lived and flourished in other countries and places before. I lived in the Philippines until I was 23 years old, when I married my American husband and decided to immigrate to the United States. I gave up all my possessions, connections, status, and power, when I moved to Dover, Delaware, to start a new life. I crammed all my material possessions in a monster suitcase on my way to my new home, halfway around the world. The blasted artifact ripped open before we reached our destination. Despite the many challenges along the way, life in Delaware, yesterday and today, has been, and continues to be, fulfilling, rich, and satisfying. I also worked and lived in Japan as an exchange administrator, and had an amazing time learning the language, the culture, the cuisine, and exploring exotic places. It was a learning experience that allowed me to grow as a leader and as a human being. I also explored living in Hawaii, where I learned that home is where my sons live. In essence, moving to a new space is nothing new or frightening to me. Perhaps my hesitation has something to do with the process of aging, where I am less willing to try new ways of living. Or my indecision could stem from lack of energy or feeling less healthy, which makes me think that I have less control over my own destiny. It has taken me six months just to research living options and assess their relative advantages and disadvantages. I feel like I am in some kind of liminal suspension, unable to make a solid choice on where I would like to live in my old age.

It should not be this hard to make a choice, I reassure myself. It's in your muscle memory—it's much like riding a bike; you have done it before; you can successfully do it again. I constantly remind myself to be grateful that I still have the freedom to choose, unlike many seniors with compromised cognitive abilities.

Besides, there are other viable choices, such as aging in place, downsizing to a smaller house near my oldest son, in addition to choices offered in a senior facility, such as independent living, assisted living, or living in a nursing home. Lovely choices.

Another Transition!

Change is a constant in everyone's life, including mine. At 80, most older adults have navigated many crises in life, overcome them, and hopefully learned from those life-changing setbacks and seismic experiences. Is this transition any different from the past ones? What is unique about this final chapter is that there are so many *unknowns,* especially to an older person whose cognitive and emotional prowess are in a state of steady decline. It is a bleak place to be—both traumatic and empowering; knowing that you have a network of beloved family and friends by your side is the plus side. Old age and death are unlike any other life transitions, where you have a one-way ticket on a jet plane to eternity—destination, unknown; departure and arrival time, unknown.

Creating New Pathways

In her book, *Pathfinders* (1981), renowned journalist and best-selling author, Gail Sheehy, "examines—through personal case histories, analysis, and examples—creative, original, and expansive ways to effectively overcome the crises of adult life by drawing on one's own inner resources, and finding a path to well-being." She refers to these individuals as "pathfinders," who refuse to surrender to life's assaults and misfortunes. She reveres them as real-life champions. She points out that pathfinders are able to navigate life's malicious streak by developing three qualities—control, confidence, and courage—which can neutralize life's challenges.

Finally, clinical psychologist and bestselling author Tara Brach, advises us in her book, *Trusting the Gold* (2021), that "When we remember the basic goodness of our Being, we open to happiness, peace, and freedom." In addition to harnessing my inner resources of resilience, confidence, and courage, I trust in the infinite goodness of life, in the *gold* within me and my network of family and friends—*my beloved community*—who love and value me. It is this sacred circle of protection that will sustain me with enduring support, love, and warmth during the fragile moments of old age and transition as I glide through the final frontier.

CHAPTER 6

Time: Why Does it Speed Up as I Am Getting Older?

TIME IS SO PRECIOUS—it is an encoded measure of our limited time on earth; it allows us to remember key moments and experiences in our lives; it challenges us to use it wisely because it's finite and limited; and it helps us to review our lives and get it in sharper focus. Yet, we have minimal proof of its concrete existence. In fact, Einstein stated, "Time is an illusion." A group of respected scientists also believes that time is an illusion, and is simply made up of human memories (Sean Carroll, *Is Time Real,* October 18, 2013). Our senses do not perceive time when it's actually happening. We can't see, touch, hear, taste, or feel time.

What Is Time?

Astrophysicist Paul Sutter (*What Is Time?* April 5, 2022) states, "Time is the apparent progression of events from past to future." Although we are able to perceive the passage of time through memories of our experiences, there are many unanswered questions about its nature and essence. For example, scientists believe that time moves only in one direction; it's a linear progression—that is it can move forward into the future, but it cannot move backwards into the past. Currently, most scientists believe that we cannot time travel into the past.

Why Does Time Appear to Move Faster as We Age?

As a youngster, I frequently got impatient and didn't quite know how to handle the incredible amount of discretionary time during summer vacations. My cousins and I engaged in a flurry of activities that challenged our creative and hungry minds and disposed of all that explosive, bottled energy. We played Monopoly, Scrabble, cards all day long. In between these passive games, we participated in active games and sports, like roller skating, fencing, basketball, and war games. We played pretend-soldiers inside real discarded tanks, remnants left by American soldiers, who defended our country during World War II. We ran wild, climbed trees and roofs, rolled dried leaves into make-believe cigarettes, and pretended to smoke them like reefers. But time appeared to be so slow, long, and unlimited. We couldn't wait to go back to school, grow up, and go to college.

Now that I am in my 80s, time appears to be moving at such a rapid and accelerated pace that I sometimes get lost in keeping up with dates and days. Days, weeks, and months seem to blend together in one linear time. I find myself lost, with barely a fleeting awareness of discrete experiences and monotonous events. I have to consciously reflect on when I did routine tasks, such as cleaning the house, doing the laundry, or paying bills. I turned around once, and my granddaughter is now a young woman! How did this happen? Where did the years go? At this advanced age, time flies, even when I am not having a good time.

Retrospective Time

Physicist, psychologists, philosophers, and other scientists have been engaged in the study of time and its nature, but no one has yet come up with a complete description of time. It's important to remember that our frame of reference in how we measure the passage of time relates to *retrospective time*—that is remembered time—not time that is actually happening in real time.

Perception of Time: Subjective Perception

The evolution or flow of time appears to be continuous and irreversible. Time is a continuum and linear; it's possible to move forward into the future, but it's not possible to move backwards or time travel into the past. The only time I experienced this deviation was when I did a past life regression with a practitioner.

Neural Transmission: How it Affects Time Perception

Scientists believe that our subjective time perception is influenced by the speed and quality of *neural transmission,* where we perceive time as moving at a slow pace as children, and then moving faster and faster as we age. Children's brains are still developing and neurons don't have all the myelin sheath that allows electrical impulses to transmit information, efficiently and quickly, along nerve cells. Dr. Patricia Costello, a neuroscientist and program director at Walden University, explains that "Children's working memory, attention, and executive function are all undergoing development at the neural circuit level." This maturation process results in a slower neural transmission, which in turn affects how they perceive time. Dr. Costello concludes that "By the time we are adults, our time circuits are done wiring and we have learned from experience how to correctly encode the passage of time."

Amygdala & Memory Formation

Another critical factor that could explain the difference in time perception between older people and children involves the amygdala, the region of the brain that makes memories. Children are constantly exposed to new ideas, new knowledge, and experiences that leave lasting impressions on their memories. It appears that memory formation is more frequent and robust during earlier years. As memories form, time feels more drawn out and protracted. In contrast, fewer new and intense memories are formed later in life, which seems to make time pass more rapidly. For some, the monotonous tempo of simply surviving old age makes the day-to-day routine of living blend into one big blur.

The amygdala is a fascinating structure, with critical and diverse functions. According to writer-editor Olivia Guy-Evans who specializes in writing about neuroscience and mental health, "The amygdala in the limbic system plays a key role in how animals assess and respond to environmental threats and challenges by evaluating the emotional importance of sensory information and prompting an appropriate response." The amygdala is an almond-shaped structure located in the medial temporal lobe, nestled in front of or anterior to the hippocampus. The hippocampus is also involved in the processing and retrieval of memories and plays a vital role in regulating learning. The main job of the amygdala is to regulate emotions, such as fear and aggression. Some scientists (Daniel Salzman, 2019) now believe that the amygdala's role in emotional information processing is not simply limited to negative emotions, such as fear, but it is also responsible for processing positive emotions, such as happiness and joy. Our knowledge base concerning this tiny but mighty brain structure is still evolving from its limited role in the processing of fear to a much wider perspective involving the regulation of both positive and negative emotions.

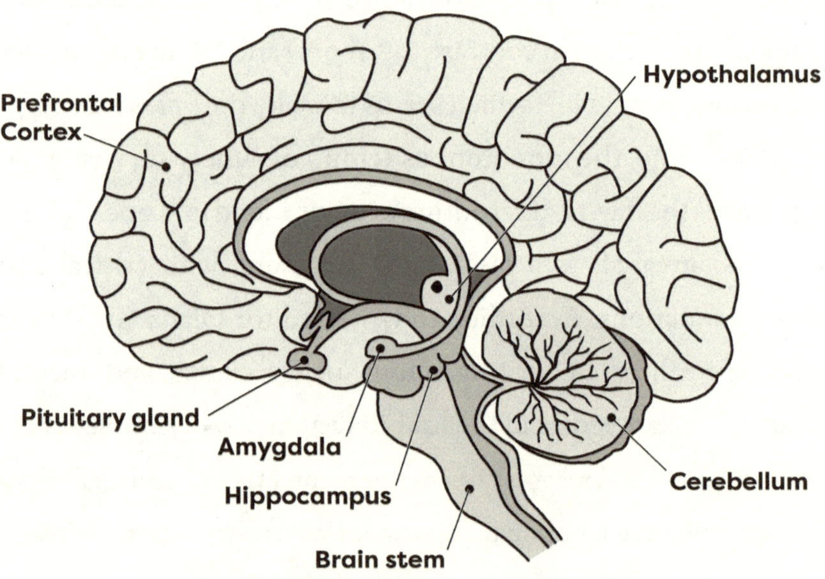

Figure 1: The Amygdala of the Brain

How Can I Recapture Lost Time?

About a decade or so ago, I wanted to recapture the lost years by doing a past life regression with a local practitioner in Odessa,

Delaware. Since we are not able to time travel into the past, despite all the cosmic buzz about virtual worlds and the metaverse, past life regression could be a viable existential choice, which does not violate the laws of physical science.

What Is Past Life Regression?

Norcross, Koocher, and Garofalo define past lives regression as "a method that uses hypnosis to recover what practitioners believe are memories of past lives or incarnations. The practice is widely considered discredited and unscientific by medical practitioners, and experts generally regard claims of recovered memories of past lives as fantasies or delusions . . ." Some therapists who employ this technique believe that mental health issues experienced by some patients might have their origins in traumatic experiences in their past lives. The purpose of the session, according to my guide, is to explore unresolved emotional problems from past lives carried on to the present lifetime, and to understand and embrace the lessons learned from past incarnations. I welcomed the session with an open mind, and plowed through the hour and a half more out of curiosity than a spiritual enlightenment of sorts.

My Experience with Past Life Regression

The past life regression guide advised me to close my eyes and imagine that I am entering a door to the past. Once I cross that threshold I will be transported into my past lives. As I crossed the boundary, I stepped out of the door and followed the light into my past. It looked like 18th-century England, somewhere in the countryside. I did not see anything at first, until midway in the regression process. Then it dawned on me that I was drowning at the bottom of a lake. I was walking leisurely around the lake when I accidentally tripped and landed in the lake. I could not swim, so I was unable to save myself. My lover, who was having a picnic with me by the lake, was unaware of what was happening to me. He blamed himself for not being able to save me, became an alcoholic, and later married a nice woman, who helped him re-shape his life. In several other incarnations, I lived in Colonial America, 18th-century France (during the Napoleonic Wars), 14th-century China, and 17th-century Japan, and in all of these lives, my partners/husbands died young. In all of my apparitions, I was always a widow and never experienced the love of that one soulmate. My major purpose in returning to this life is to look for my one true love, my soulmate, who in this present lifetime is married to another woman and has a teenage son. Well, how can anyone not be enticed to recapture a past life as rich, exotic, and transcendent as this one? This is one whimsical way of extending time and elongating memories of times past, and it cost me less than $100.

Now what other practical ways can we explore to maximize the time we have left and live it to the fullest? Here's a listing of creative but practical ways of capturing time:

- **Passion and purpose:** Engaging in meaningful activities, like doing work or volunteer work to serve others and your community is a good first step. It's also important to find out what your talents and abilities are, what you're good at, so you can deploy and harness those abilities to the optimum level. How do I find out what my quintessential strengths are? Whenever I do executive and employee coaching, I always ask my clients to write down their strengths and weaknesses. For the first trial run, I ask them to write down what comes to mind intuitively. A week or so later, I instruct them to reflect on their choices, and apply their signature strengths to a job that they are passionate about. One of my clients used this simple technique to come up with a career that made her happy and fulfilled. Of course, finding out what you're good at, applying those skills to a job or engaging in volunteer work, requires more than a 10-minute exercise. It takes time and effort to come up with a viable choice.

The self is fluid and elastic and can be molded and shaped to be in harmony with the ever-changing demands of every cycle of your life. What makes you feel alive? What do you love to do? These are questions with evolving answers as we learn and grow. Knowing who you are, your purpose and your passion, are crucial in using your limited time on earth to the fullest. Life is short and death is long. So live life with passion.

- Keeping a journal and a happiness folder: I maximize happy times by writing about happy and memorable events in my sometimes daily but mostly weekly journal. I also note down the negative emotions and experiences to learn and grow. I also keep a "Happiness Folder," where I collect greeting cards, notes, email messages, letters, and other correspondence that relay positive messages and inspire pleasurable emotions and feelings in me. I recycle the joy juices that I experienced the first time when I read my journal or plow through files of happy messages. Dr. Stefan Klein (*The Science of Happiness,* 2006) reminds us that "It isn't enough to be happy. We have to be aware of our happiness . . . Satisfaction is like a mosaic created out of many happy moments." I savor this pleasant feeling of well-being and happiness by re-experiencing the happy moments as many times in my lifetime as I choose. This way, I get to savor and relish the positive feelings that I experienced the first time around—a simple but smart way of prolonging happy times and elongating your discretionary time.

- Keeping a folder of photos and videos: The concept is similar to the simple technique above of keeping a journal and a happiness folder. These steps allow you to recapture the pleasurable experiences, record them in your amygdala, and later retrieve the happy memories during your leisure time.

Having a video of the event or experience is even more powerful because you can experience it again in living color, and it stimulates all five basic senses. Repeated viewing of the event or experience might even create new neural pathways, if you learn new concepts and remember new information. As artist-photographer Katie Thurmes reminds us "We take photos [and videos] as a return ticket to a moment otherwise gone." It's a win-win!

- Traveling: Traveling is important to build strong and resilient connections among people from diverse backgrounds by learning about their cultures, music, food, and the way they live. It's the best real-time education and respite that nurtures your mind, body, and soul. Some of the most memorable, relaxing, fun times I have ever had were spent visiting foreign countries and different states in the United States. It gave me a chance to be fully engaged and forget the worries and challenges of my life, and not be bound by time or space. Chief Seattle of the Duwamish and Suquamish tribes cautions us to "Take only memories, leave only footprints" when we travel and go on vacations.

Time, it is so precious. Let's remember to look back at the past with satisfaction, seize, enjoy and savor the present moment, and look to the future with optimism and joy.

CHAPTER 7

Let the Light In

A RAGING PANDEMIC, an economy in shambles, and a volatile racial divide—all are prima facie evidence of the maliciousness of life. We have national leaders who are bumbling their way towards untested and sometimes delusional solutions, and even worse, fanning the flames of injustice and conflict to divide and conquer. To top it all, both leaders and followers are confused about facts, data, and the truth. The guiding moral compass, entrenched in the distant past, has been all but forgotten; a temporary state of chaos and confusion reigns. Truth decay (Kavanagh & Rich, 2018) has become the operating transactional template—the increasing blurring of lines between facts and opinions, and it appears that the truth does not even matter anymore. This seems to be the guiding spirit of the day—from fake news and media outlets, to social media tweets, right up to the primal source of misinformation at the federal seat of power and governance.

You lost your job. Your parents are seriously sick with the COVID-19 virus. And you're feuding with your co-workers and neighbors on who should be president of this country. There is wholesale chaos, hatred, and discontent everywhere. How then can I ask you to reflect, to celebrate, and to be thankful for your fragile and seemingly hopeless life?

Now, all these catastrophic events are not historical anomalies. Humans have experienced all these tragedies and challenges before. The Bubonic Plague, a global pandemic that struck Europe and Asia in the 1350s, was responsible for the death of one-third of the world's population. It caused France and England to declare a truce and halt the Hundred Years War, destroyed the British feudal system, and stopped the Vikings from further exploration of Greenland and North America. The Black Plague returned with a vengeance in the early 1700s. Then, there was the 1918–1919 flu pandemic that caused the death of an estimated fifty million people worldwide and 675,000 Americans. Life and death, health and sickness, economic prosperity and downturn are all part and parcel of the cycle of life. It's the yin yang paradigm that represents all the opposing forces and principles in the universe—an inevitable and eternal cycle of reversal because every principle has the seeds of its opposite embedded in its essence. For example, politician A is thrilled and deliriously happy because he won the election today. Fast-forward two years from now, he would suffer a devastating defeat, which would make him unhappy and beaten down. All these and more are integral parts of the oneness and unity of life.

As I was writing this book, I took a break by enjoying the view from my office back window. I saw bright and scintillating rays of sunlight filtering through the leaves of the trees in my backyard. The Japanese calls this phenomenon, *Komorebi.* I thought about this emerging light as a precursor of positive events that are now occurring and are primed to occur. There is reasonable hope for a less divided and more unified populace; two promising new vaccines, with between 90 to close to 95 percent effectiveness; record numbers of Americans engaged in the democratic process by exercising their right to vote. There are reasons to stay positive and be grateful for the forward movement that's slowly gracing our barren wasteland. Although there are many problems that remain to be resolved, there are significant changes that we need to celebrate and be thankful for.

A democracy is not a spectator sport; it requires active engagement and action from the body politic. Our experiment in democracy can only survive and thrive if we have an informed and active electorate and leaders who possess the right combination of character and competency. As a citizen and a resident of this great country, how can you contribute and be an architect of the freedom and liberation that we aspire to? Beyond the election, get involved and engaged in your communities. Try to focus on things you can control and be part of the solution. What are you passionate about; what gives your life vigor and renewed purpose? For example, I try to spend valuable time supporting women's issues, assisting people with disabilities, and engaging in lifelong learning working with libraries. Find your path and follow your bliss!

Sometimes the suggested prescription to neutralize the present problems are simple and ordinary, but tested remedies. They are not high-tech innovations, but common remedies and relatively inexpensive. For example, to stem the rising tide of the COVID-19 virus, we are asked by our leaders to wear masks, maintain a physical distance of six feet, and frequently wash our hands. We are requested to voluntarily comply to promote the common good, not to deliberately squash our individual freedoms. These steps have been adopted in Asian countries, like South Korea and Japan, with miraculous outcomes. We're called upon to sacrifice just a little bit longer. These preventive steps remind me of what my doctor told me during my annual physical exam. She shared with me that because of my diet and exercise, I have an enviable cholesterol level, which is typically found among much younger cohorts. Simple steps like a diet rich in vegetables and just walking a single mile a day are part of the secret sauce. She also noted that drinking a glass of red wine probably helped. And I completely agreed!

Edward Felsenthal, editor-in-chief of *Time* magazine aptly concluded in his recent editorial (*Time,* November 23, 2020), "Our dueling realities remain. Biden and Harris, and all of us, have much work ahead." With this awareness in mind and having taken the first step, we deserve to take a little breather. Pause. Reflect. Celebrate. Give thanks!

CHAPTER 8

Grief, Hope, and Transformation

TODAY IS EXACTLY A MONTH since my younger brother Sonny died. I am still in a state of disbelief and confusion, tinged with anger at my powerlessness against life's maliciousness. How can this be? I just had a long and interesting conversation with him less than a month before he had a massive heart attack and died, just like that! He and his wife were celebrating their 50th wedding anniversary in Switzerland and Italy, when this gruesome event occurred. It was supposed to be a dance of celebration, not a dance of death. It was an unexpected event—Sonny was healthy, full of life, and younger than three of his four living siblings.

Grief

What is grief: Dr. William Smith states (*The Psychology of Grief,* June 20, 2021) that . . . "grief is an intense emotional experience triggered by a loss . . . and commonly experienced in the context of death." For my siblings and me, the debilitating feeling of grief was doubly as intense and difficult to process because Sonny was younger and more physically fit than we are. The death of a sibling also reminds us of our own mortality. However, the unexpected nature of death is a fundamental reality that affects all human beings. The stunning swiftness and finality of death makes it seem surreal and fictitious. For example, I had a meeting with my friend Larry just a couple of days before he died. He looked well, healthy, and hopeful. Three days later, he was gone. I had a similar experience with my sister Lita. We had a delightful conversation during the holidays and before her birthday. A week or so later, she was completely unavailable and unreachable. She was, unequivocally and instantaneously, gone.

Five stages of grief: Kubler-Ross (*Death and Dying,* 1969) proposed the classic five stages of grief primarily based on the experiences of individuals facing their own death. My initial experience seems to follow the first three stages of *Denial, Anger,* *and Bargaining* in my first month of grieving for my brother's death. However, my experience of the three first stages is not linear, but more of a continuum—a recurring experience that keeps on going and changes slowly over time. When the feelings are ignited, they seem to occur simultaneously. I feel the shock, the disbelief, and the confusion all at the same time. My first reaction is more of disbelief rather than denial. Denial rejects the truth outright, whereas with disbelief, the truth is accessible to me but it just does not seem to make sense.

I just spoke with Sonny two days before he died. He was alive and kicking. When my cousin called to share the dreadful news, I shouted in disbelief, "No, no, no, not Sonny!" This feeble truth does not align with my recent reality. It seems like an illusion; an imaginary tale. Experts on death and grief affirm that the cluster feelings of denial, disbelief, and shock are often the first reactions to the unimaginable reality of death. This initial reaction is a protective mechanism that allows individuals to absorb the reality gradually, process it at their own pace, and ultimately come to grips with it.

I experienced *Bargaining* more acutely when my husband died at a young age in 1979. I distinctly remember driving through the inner city of Wilmington, Delaware, and pleading with God to let my husband live. I yelled at the universe and asked "Why me? Why don't you take that addict sitting on the cold pavement, right there, snorting cocaine?" I also asked for a little miracle and promised to attend church service again, if God would let my husband live. But, my pleading fell on deaf ears—my husband died anyway a few months later. After he died, grieving was a luxury since I had two kids to raise, and a new job—where I needed to learn new competencies and perform at my level best so I could pass the probationary period. And there were innumerable other tasks that needed to be completed when a spouse dies unexpectedly.

I experienced *Depression,* the fourth stage, about a year after the death of my husband. This was the longest stage for me since the emotion affected my physical and mental health. I got sick with a serious flu and was unable to cope with the enormity of the loss. It was a challenging and dark period because I was beginning to accept the reality that my husband, the love of my life, was forever gone. With my brother's death, I have not seen the ugly specter of depression yet; it has only been a month since his death.

I failed to experience authentic *Acceptance* when my husband died until I faced and embraced the pain that devoured my soul. Acceptance was a soul snuffer—affirming reality meant that my love was absolutely and totally gone—forever. However, embracing the truth, going through unfathomable pain, and taking nourishment from the darkness that surrounded me were the only pathways to redemption or at least a temporary amnesty from sorrow and pain.

Transformation: adapting to a new life: Stage 6? There were a significant number of respondents in my survey of people who live alone (due to widowhood, separation, or divorce), who managed to transcend the grief of separation and death, and come out balanced and happy *(SoloPower: How to Harness the Secret Energy of Living Alone,* 2014). Sixty-four percent responded that they were either happy (41 percent) or very happy (23 percent) most or all the time, which is contrary to common perceptions. Friends and acquaintances who approached me for advice and mentoring after widowhood also disclosed that they were fairly happy, once they accepted the reality of the loss and adapted to a new way of life. The resulting resilience, self-knowledge, and transformation are the by-products of acceptance—that is acknowledging the loss and feeling the resulting pain as part of the recovery process. I recommend that we add *Stage 6: Transformation: Adapting to a New Life* as the final stage of the grief process. I suspect that for some, maybe even most people who experience grief and loss, there is a gradual journey of recovery that could culminate in self-growth and transformation.

Grief cycle: I believe that grief is a cyclical process, where individuals experience the same phase multiple times, as they move on their gradual journey towards healing and wholeness. They pivot back and forth between the different stages, as they forge less tenuous and stronger bonds, build resilience and coping skills, and better connect and identify with an aspirational present and future.

Hope: A Protective Armor and a Pathway

What is hope and why is it critical for our well-being? Chan Hellman, founding director of the Hope Research Center at the University of Oklahoma states *(Time: Five Ways to Cultivate Hope When You Don't Have Any,* November 20, 2023) that it is "the belief or the expectation that the future can be better, and that more importantly, we have the capacity to pursue the future." Hope is a key ingredient in our ability to survive and flourish even during times of turbulence and tragedies. It affects our levels of well-being, motivation, and performance. Shane Lopez, a senior scientist at Gallup, defines hope as "the belief that the future will be better than the present, coupled with the belief that you have the power to make it so." Much like Hellman's definition, the power of hope lies in our capacity to manage the future in areas that we can control. Unlike death itself, we have a *choice* in how we shape our desired future—we can develop plans, set goals, and act decisively to define a brighter future for ourselves, as we manage, adapt, and live in a new altered life.

Dr. Dan J. Tomasulo *(The Power of Hope,* May 2023) points out that "People high in hope have sustainably better physical and mental well-being. They also tend to live longer and happier lives. High-hope people see and respond to the world differently, and they use their thoughts to focus on what they can control." Hope, a positive emotion, offers individuals a *protective armor* against the unpredictability and challenges of life. Hope also inspires people to see possibilities instead of simply challenges and risks, and this perspective allows them to carve out new and creative pathways to a new way of living. They are not only persistent, but they are also tenacious. Tenacity requires them to use new information to find new pathways to achieving their goals. In the persistence mode, individuals have a short-sighted focus on a single solution, which they attempt to apply repeatedly until it works. There is creativity, passion, and renewed zest in being hopeful. The negative energy expended while coping with grief can be repurposed and transformed into a new creative tension capable of transforming lives.

Transformation

Sonny was a little philosopher, even at age four. He and I would sit on the floor of our living room in Quezon City, lean against the sofa, and discuss the meaning of life, death, and other universal realities. We continued this intimate discussion on life, love, politics, and other crucial topics throughout our lives. A couple of weeks before Sonny died, we had a long and meaningful conversation about life and purpose, much like when we were children, just welcoming life with innocence and promise. He thoughtfully reflected on his life's accomplishments, and did a careful inventory of his triumphs and defeats. He was always guided by the steely determination to do good and to help others and his community. He knew his value, but there were experiences with a handful of friends and relatives that he failed to understand. I reassured him that no one is capable of pleasing everyone and that the burden is on them, not on him. I reiterated my belief in him and his goodness, and recounted how I could not have survived the untimely death of my husband without him by my side. He and my dad became the father figures in our lives. He was and will remain a towering figure in my life.

Close to the end of our conversation, he reminded me to consider writing a chapter about *Kintsugi,* the Japanese art of repairing broken pottery by putting the pieces together with epoxy-laced gold, silver, or platinum to create something stronger and more beautiful. At a deeper level, this concept can be applied to life, especially when someone you love and cherish dies unexpectedly. It is a message from the grave that I am shining a light on to help our family, our community, and our friends heal, grow, and transcend this stunning grief. If shattered pieces of a once beautiful work of art can be creatively put back together to give birth to a new masterpiece, maybe our broken hearts and minds can gently be weaned off Sonny's glow, and survive and thrive by embracing the legacy he left behind. Sonny left the world indelible footprints on the sands of time, which will remain intact for all eternity.

Here's poem, in honor of Sonny's memory:

Ode to Kintsugi

In life's mosaic, let our fractured hearts mend,
With golden threads, resilience blends.
Embrace the broken pieces
that reform and transform.
A poetic dance that gives one a chance,
To embrace the grace of a new and vibrant life.

CHAPTER 9

An Attitude of Gratitude

The Menschen in My Life

I WOULD LIKE TO GREET this season of thanksgiving, grace, and renewal with an attitude of gratitude—a clear acknowledgement and deep appreciation of the gifts bestowed on me by family, friends, and acquaintances, and sometimes, by strangers.

I consider my newfound friend Kevin to be a real mensch. According to Dr. Saul Levine (*Psychology Today,* November 19, 2015), "a mensch refers to a person of intrinsic worth, a decent, thoughtful individual. It is a Yiddish word . . . to describe a very special person . . . one who manifested and exuded certain admirable traits." Kevin is a man of integrity, honesty, compassion, and kindness. My first encounter with him was through my bay window in my living room. When the pandemic started in 2020 and I was caged inside the house, I felt liberated when looking through glass doors and windows. I accidentally peeped through that huge window and spotted Kevin picking up my garbage bin, which I failed to move towards the curb so he could easily dump the contents down the chute of his truck. He got off his driver seat and pulled my heavy trash bin towards his truck, unloaded the refuse, and rolled it back towards the garage. Then he waved at me, I waved back and bowed to say thanks. From that point on, I waited for his truck to roll into the neighborhood to greet him with a bow and a whispered thank-you, while he waved back at me, and nodded, with his hands clasped together. This was our ritual tableau—our sign language communication that went on for a year until I was able to get my COVID-19 vaccine. We met face to face for the first time and I thanked him for his kindness and thoughtfulness. I told him that I waited for him every Thursday so I could connect with another human being other than my Zoom colleagues. Surprisingly, I was also a bright light to him during these dark months of pandemic isolation. He told me that he looked forward to stopping by my house to connect non-verbally, which sustained him during the monotonous days of the pandemic, where everyone was walled-in.

Amie is a consummate mensch, who delights and finds fulfillment in helping others. She has rescued me many times in the past, but her support and assistance are life-saving during this pandemic. I have been unable to drive for months on end because of a vestibular problem, and Amie is always there to take me to the many doctors and specialists, to go to the supermarkets and drugstores, and to simply be there to listen and to socialize. She is Dover's one-woman social service agency, who helps every individual who needs support, assistance, and advocacy, and she does it all without expecting anything in return. She holds up more than half the sky for hundreds of people in this little town. She is a virtual superhero, a consummate mensch!

The Meal on Wheels program, administered through the Modern Maturity Center, has been a life-saving service for me and the many homebound seniors in the area. Under the able leadership of Trudie, the program provides nutritious meals to close to 1,000 seniors in the city of Dover and adjacent communities. Two volunteers stand out in their ability to connect, serve, and elevate the spirit of the senior citizens with their customer-focused service and caring. The first one is Keith, who lived in New Jersey for many years and moved to Delaware when he retired. He is patient, jovial, and is a giant, both figuratively and literally. He is tall and has a big and caring heart. He rings the doorbell and lies in wait until I show up. He doesn't just leave the bag of food on the table on the front steps of my house, but he waits to make sure that I am all right. He told me that part of his job, which he considers a sacred covenant, is to make certain that all is well with me. A wonderful side benefit of the service is the potential to carry on a real conversation with a live person—a delight for the human sensory system that has not been used and lies quietly, waiting silently like a coiled cobra ready to be called into action. Leon is the other volunteer who has been a real lifeline to me during the pandemic. He is sharp, a lifelong learner, service-oriented, and actively promotes equity and racial justice for all. He engages my mind with his insights and deep understanding of political, social, and economic issues affecting ordinary citizens. He sends carefully crafted letters to public servants to make them accountable to the people they serve. He is an active participant, not merely a spectator in the democratic process. He is a beacon in the darkness, attempting to build a bridge to a just and more equitable country. It's a real joy to carry on lively life-changing conversations with Leon, a certifiable mensch!

Finally, survival in a tough and altered future is impossible, challenging at best, without the support and caring of a strong and loving family. One loving son ministers and nurtures to my survival needs for food and sustenance, and will search to the ends of the earth to find what I love to eat and drink—my staple snack of saltine mini-crackers, my healthy green tea beverage loaded with antioxidants, and my life-sustaining spring water. The other loving son listens with intention, suggests poetry and prose that nourishes my mind and soul, and infuses my beaten-down psyche with courage and determination. He does not enable, but dares me to push the boundaries and join the fellowship, joy, and revelry of the unfamiliar social landscape and workplace that I deserted many moons ago. Recently, he sent me a link to this notable Nigerian poet named Ijeoma Umebinyuo, who jump-started my healing and recovery with these powerful lines:

> *Start now. Start where you are. Start with fear. Start with pain. Start with doubt. Start with hands shaking. Start with voice trembling but start. Start where you are, with what you have. Just . . . start.*

We can flourish and grow with family on our side, a tribal community collectively unfolding its complicated sparkle, and a united country, tolerant of its conflicting realities. Despite hard times, most of us have a wonderful life, with a mensch or two by our side. Let us give thanks!

PART 2

For Communities and the Larger Society

CHAPTER 10

The Social Justice Conundrum

WHY IS OUR COUNTRY facing a racial reckoning, a clamor for gender equality, an upsurge of violence, and demands for social justice in every facet of our lives? All these and more are happening during a worldwide health pandemic, which thankfully, appears to be subsiding. Perhaps, the recent police brutalities against George Floyd, Ahmaud Arbery, Breonna Taylor, and half a dozen more people of color, brought the issue of racial injustice to the forefront. The tolerance level of the oppressed reached a boiling point and it broke the dam of fear and submission. Granted, the collective hibernation and reaction could have been affected, even peripherally, by the political and social chaos that plagued the country before, during, and after the election. The people were on lockdown at home and maybe, this respite from ordinary life and work provided them with the needed discretionary time to reflect on fundamental existential issues of purpose and passion. Human beings are born free and no one can cage the yearning for freedom forever.

In the biological world, comparable events happen to species called punctuated equilibrium. It is an evolutionary theory that claims that the evolution of species displays a characteristic pattern of short periods of rapid and intense change, followed by long periods of no change—referred to as stasis or equilibrium (https://biologydictionary.net/punctuated-equilibrium). My fear is that rapid, positive changes will occur, just like in the natural world, then we will forget about the issues for another half a century or so. We talked about racial equality in the 1960s and passed the Civil Rights amendments, and became aware of the need for women's liberation in the 1970s, which commitment didn't resurface until recently. We talk more than we act—we need both dreamers and doers who ACT.

It's important to remember that social justice problems are all interconnected, what social scientists call the *intersectionality* of social problems. For example, at the systemic level, we cannot address racial injustice unless we factor in how race affects the economic, health, educational, social, and technological issues, all intertwined with racial injustice. This points to the complexity of prejudices and the convergence among these factors. At the individual level, in addition to assessing how racial inequity affects a woman of color, we also need to factor in how her gender, age, educational level, class, and other demographic markers further exacerbate her disadvantages. We need to be aware and to truly understand the complexity of the multiple inequities and discriminations that she has to face.

What are possible solutions to these intractable social justice problems? Social justice problems are systemic and require a systemic solution—a deliberate, planned, holistic, and sustained solution that requires the continuing commitment of both citizens and leaders. To mitigate the problem, we need both individual and collective commitment and action. We might not be able to solve systemic problems of this proportion, but at least we can marshal our people and financial resources to mitigate the problem and achieve some significant movement in the equity agenda. How do we move the needle forward? At the moment, we appear to be simply dealing with the manifestations of the racial injustice problem that can be seen and perceived by our untrained eyes and senses. The surface of the iceberg is visible, real, and compelling. Seeing George Floyd gasping for air, begging for his life for nine solid minutes, depicts a palpable canvas of how this society values Black lives. We have to dig deep into the subterranean iceberg of American history to uncover the roots of this systemic racism. How do we melt away centuries of racism, injustice, and inhumanity to our fellow human beings? Remember, we have experienced similar rumblings, awakenings, and enlightenments before—from slavery, to reconstruction, to segregation—when Blacks were granted freedom, the dominant race simply built barriers to maintain its control and dominance. Let me say it again, we have been down this path before, searing moments of reckoning, attempting to change the paradigm, and then losing steam to follow through on promises, legislation, and enforcement. Then we relax in the stable niche of the familiar and preferential power paradigm.

Maybe we can start with influencing the conscious *mind,* before working on the uncompromising *heart.* Here's an actionable suggestion: Can we teach African American history in schools, or make certain that history books include this major omission? Also, historians and other scholars need to rewrite and review the accuracy of facts included in this historical revision. For example, I took Black History at the graduate school at Washington College, but I never read or learned about the Tulsa Massacre. It's only lately that mainstream American learned of this major human tragedy of Black extermination.

Is it possible that we treated slaves not simply as less than human, but also with less concern and emotional attachment than we valued our properties and financial investments? Is this an indication of a deep-seated national character flaw that we hold secretly and unconsciously within our hearts? We might not even be aware of it. It's reflexive, automatic, and almost an instinctive reaction that has been the result of centuries of socialization and acculturation. I wonder if our society's attitudes towards women is governed by the same instinctive process. Think about it when you're cutting grass or doing the laundry.

In my executive coaching practice, I try not to have a contract with any leader who is not open to learning or one who feels that she does not need coaching because she is a good leader, has all the right competencies, and does not need to change or tweak anything about her leadership skills. We might need the same reflection, awareness, and attitudinal change to occur before we begin the healing process and the solution phase of this national crisis. We need to think, reflect, and begin to understand the key role of these existential questions.

Is this who we are as a nation? Who are we? Is this predisposition towards superiority and social injustice a part of our national character, our cultural heritage—deeply embedded in our value system? Why are we doing what we're doing? We all need to reflect, individually and collectively, on these realities before we can forge ahead and be part of the solution.

CHAPTER 11

The Oppression of Asian Americans

Exploring My Own Truth

FOR A COUPLE OF WEEKS NOW, I have been reflecting on my experiences in this country as an Asian American—the discriminations I faced, the support and friendship I received, why I reacted the way I did, and how these touch points in my life influenced who I am today. Preparing to participate as a panel member for the Delaware Division of Human Relations motivated me to reflect more deeply than I ever did before about this segment of my life. Initially, the challenges didn't really appear to affect me that much since I have to consciously recall them to engender any kind of coherent and muscular emotion.

I tried to create a neutral space in my heart and allow the difficult emotions to surface. I thought that most of the encounters were simply subtle acts of discrimination; nothing really violent or dehumanizing. I was dead wrong! Some of my experiences were brazen, hateful, and not so-subtle acts of discrimination and prejudice.

When I first came to America, I was greeted by one of my husband's relatives with an unwelcome request to my husband to leave me. No reason given. It was simply a coercive, surprising comment from someone I had not even met. I never ever thought of myself as unworthy, so I just dismissed her ridiculous request. I honestly thought the guy was truly lucky to have me. Despite the poverty of her expectations, I remained unflappable, and was shielded by my belief in my own uniqueness and self-worth—thanks to my mother, who raised me to be self-reliant, resilient, and strong. I did not need permission from anyone to be proud of who I am. I simply ignored her, until later on she came around and decided to accept me for who I am.

Five years later, my husband and I bought a house in a subdivision west of Dover, Delaware. I learned a couple of years later that the neighbors were informally surveyed if they would mind having an "educated Asian" move into *their* neighborhood.

That was in the early 1970s. The most disturbing incident in my experience as an immigrant occurred in this neighborhood. A neighbor who lived about a block away from our house started getting uncomfortable with my presence in the same contiguous space. I can't distinctly remember what precipitated her racist comments because she was initially friendly and open. I vaguely remember an instance when I didn't comply with her request, and she got irritated and barked at me "to get back where I came from!" I didn't want to further exacerbate the situation so I simply stared sharply at her and left. I supposed I just didn't think highly of her, and felt that she wasn't really worthy of my energy and attention. It was when she started bullying my son, and attempted to run over us while we were doing our walks that I fought back and took her to court. It was a traumatic event that I probably buried in my conscious mind all these years. The anger and frustration that radiated through my soul came cascading back through time and space. The singular act of racism and inhumanity enraged me. I am a reasonable and rational person. I don't look for trouble or engage in small disagreements. I know how to carry on difficult conversations, address problems, compromise, and come up with reasonable solutions. I don't easily engage in conflict, but I set boundaries and when you cross that line I am ready for whatever tricks you have. I am not afraid of conflict. We won the case and she was fined and ordered to stay away from us. I always look for light in the darkness, and this experience taught me how to better value my heritage, my culture, my family, and myself.

I have also been the beneficiary of stunning acts of kindness and love in this sweet spot. When I had surgery, a kind neighbor brought me lunch for a week or so. A neighbor who became a friend edited one of my books, despite the fact that she was terminally ill with cancer. Another neighbor-friend taught me how to appreciate the beauty of nature, and went on relaxing walks with me through the lush vegetation and forest of our slice of paradise. Recently, a group of neighbors cleared my driveway of ten feet of snow, and periodically checks on how I am doing and if I need any food or supplies from the supermarket.

Life in the United States was smooth sailing from that point on. I encountered little, subtle, and annoying acts of racism and prejudice, which I tried to neutralize with humor, laughter, and pathos. Here are a few of the typical, garden-variety type of discriminations that I encountered in my personal and professional life: being asked to sit in the back of restaurants, near the kitchen; medical professionals and customer service folks discussing issues that affect me with my husband, instead of addressing the relevant issues with me; and being mistaken as the secretary instead of the boss. A couple of years ago, I interviewed a young woman for a vacancy within our PR department. She had great credentials, interviewed fairly well, and would have been a promising candidate for the job. I took a leisurely walk with her through the corridors to see her out, as I typically do with job applicants after an interview. I find that applicants relax, soar free of their other persona, and are themselves. The applicant nicely remarked and pleasantly asked me "Why is it that you people get all the best jobs in this town?" Stunning question.

A Novel Experience—Racism

I did not experience any type of differential treatment because of the color of my skin until I immigrated to this country. Of course, there was prejudice and discrimination in my country of birth based on other identifiers, such as social class, education, money, status, and power. I was lucky to have been born into a privileged class, so racism was an unknown entity to me. It was exotic, unfamiliar, and I thought it was always directed at the Black race. To further confuse the issue, I am whiter than most White people! Many times, I might have been a victim or a target of a racist comment, but I just failed to perceive it as such. It's just like speaking a foreign language; it was an unfamiliar sound and vibration to me. My senses weren't attuned to its decibels. After all, I belonged to the upper class, so I am protected and valued by my people. I failed to realize that I am living in a different cultural milieu governed by a new set of rules, folkways, and mores.

Yes, Theresa, you are now a citizen of the United States of America, where your position as a privileged woman of status and leisure are not recognized, and the transactional nature of that prerogative is no longer legal tender. You're an Asian American, a minority in a predominantly White Anglo-Saxon America, endowed with freedom and equality, if you belong to the dominant race. What an astonishing revelation! I have lived in this country for fifty-five years, more than half a century adjusting to the American way of life. Although I perceive myself as one, and I am proud to be an American, the dominant society still sees me as an outsider, at best.

Core Problems

First and foremost, it's important to identify what the core problems are. In our haste to address the problems, we fail to identify the nature and essence of the problems. We are blinded by our visceral anger, disgust, and disbelief that racism still lives in the supposedly greatest democracy in the world. This self-consecration serves as a major barrier in seeing the problems, which at times are right in front of us. We are flawed as individuals and a nation, and collectively we have to recognize that there is a problem. We are not looking for anyone to blame, we simply would like to grow and continuously improve who we are.

Oppression of non-whites: We need to shift our paradigm to build a healthier and more just society for all. Yes, our history demonstrates the deep-seated feelings of superiority against Black Americans, Native Americans, and Asian Americans.

Collectively, we judge people by the color of their skin and their identifying facial features. Let's turn our focus on the discrimination experienced by Asian Americans in this country. There seems to be a clear-cut pattern that emerges whenever there is a complex set of economic and political threats facing the nation—we look for a scapegoat to blame instead of addressing the problem, and we invariably change the narrative. The former president used his office to shift blame for his incompetence and lack of planning by calling the coronavirus the "Chinese virus." It is sanctioned bigotry that a critical mass of vulnerable and unthinking individuals were just too quick to accept, with no empirical evidence because it fits their worldview. We have to stop labelling individuals who judiciously, patiently, and clearly show demonstrable evidence of a national malaise as "unpatriotic" or barking at them to "go back where you came from!" First of all, we are all from somewhere, the only original settlers and residents of this country are the Native Americans. Secondly, it's an ultimate act of love and loyalty to be committed to improving the value system and cultural mores of a country they love. It's called "Tough Love."

Model minority myth—speak up and act: Part of the responsibility falls on us, Asian Americans. We cannot keep silent, refuse to get involved, and refrain from acting on probable solutions. Find your voice, speak up when your civil rights are violated, and act courageously—be part of the solution. Be a beacon in the darkness, instead of hiding in the shadows. Individually, we might bumble our way through, but collectively, we could be a powerful and transformative force. As notable author Ryan Holiday reminds us, "Cancel your captivity. You have the power. Seize it."

The model minority label sounds positive and endearing on the surface. There is a tacit assumption among members of the dominant society that Asian Americans are hardworking, law-abiding, compliant, and silent. Nice compliment, but the intention is not at all pure or unselfish—it's a powerful positive reinforcement to keep the captive minority in chains, while creating conflict and negative competition among minorities, especially between Asian Americans and Black Americans. It's Machiavellian trickery, as old as the Roman Empire, intended to divide and conquer. Lastly, it is a creative and smart strategy of maintaining order, discipline, and dominance.

Possible Solutions

This is an endemic social justice problem that requires a systemic approach. What are some reasonable solutions to these seemingly confounding social justice problems? We must remember racism is a systemic problem that requires a systemic solution—a planned, intentional, and strategic solution that demands the continuing commitment of both citizens and leaders. To mitigate this complex problem involves individual and collective commitment and action. We need to find light in the darkness through collaboration and partnership with other oppressed minorities; engage the dominant society (after all, they are the gatekeepers who can open the golden doors for us) in crucial conversations; push for inclusion instead of exclusion; integrate Asian and Black history into the public schools' curricula; and push for action-oriented social justice legislation. We are at an existential crossroads—we can minimize the life suffering that goes on from generation to generation and marshal our resources to move the needle forward.

At the higher, more strategic level, we need to have leaders who have a clear vision of how to shape our future, supported by a committed citizenry, and dedicated to finding long-term solutions to these problems. Let's also make sure to engage in strategic and operational planning, identify smart and measurable goals, collect the vital few data to make certain that we are on the right track to implement mid-course corrections, and validate concrete outcomes. At the more practical and actionable levels, here are a few recommendations: Include the study of Asian history in our public schools and postsecondary school curricula; revise historical textbooks to include Asian American history, culture, and contributions of this demographic cohort; actively collaborate and support other minority groups; and get involved in addressing racial issues and conflict, to name a few.

Inclusion of Asian American history and culture as a required subject in elementary and secondary schools, postsecondary institutions, and other educational systems might sound like a simple and insignificant solution to a complex and intractable problem, but its benefits are immeasurable. Consider the positive effects of learning and the resulting behavioral change among children and young adults, when exposed to the rich history and cultural heritage of their classmates—whose roots and heritage have been a blank slate to them. Research (John H. Byrne, 2008) validates the robust formation of new neurons, which occurs at a higher rate in early years and appears to continue throughout adulthood, even in old age. Formation of new neurons in the hippocampus, which are two small seahorse-shaped regions in the brain, affects learning and memory. Neurogenesis, the process of forming new neurons, can greatly influence the speed of learning and memory retrieval.

Imagine the vast galaxy of neurons forming that could allow people to learn new, credible information, capable of changing minds and modifying behavior.

Parting Words

We have to create space and time in our hearts and minds to make this collective commitment to improve race relations, justice, and equity for all. We have to remember the interconnected nature of all social justice problems, what social scientists call the intersectionality of social problems. For example, at the strategic level, we cannot address racial injustice unless we factor in how race affects the economic, health, educational, social, housing, technological issues—all fundamentally intertwined with racial injustice. This points to the complexity of prejudices that creates overlapping systems of discriminations.

Asian hate is not simply an isolated and esoteric phenomenon. To fully understand and appreciate the deep impact of Asian discrimination on the individual—the person—we have to factor in not only her race, but also gender, economic status, level of education, social class and other identifiers.

By factoring in the interconnected nature of racism, we can better grasp the uniqueness, the visceral pain, and the devastating effects of xenophobic violence. Poet Ijeoma Umebinyuo captured the survival need to belong in these deeply moving lines:

So, here you are
too foreign for home
too foreign for here.
Never enough for both.

It's important to keep in mind that now is an opportune time to seize the moment. The recent pandemic and the ensuing violence are strong catalysts for change. We don't need to create a "burning platform" to generate chaos and dissatisfaction with the existing racial justice model. Leaders have to paint a vision of a better place, clearly explain the compelling imperative for change, and define how we can best achieve our goals.

Whatever positive action we choose to take might seem like an inconsequential spit in the ocean of hatred, but it's still a forward movement that might neutralize the racial justice ecosystem. Even the slightest movement of a pebble can create a seismic impact on the landscape. Let's forge ahead and create positive change, much like the loving kindness that I experience in my own neighborhood. Namaste!

CHAPTER 12

A New Power Model
Character-Driven Leadership

SOME SECTIONS IN THIS CHAPTER are excerpts from our book, *Women Powered! A New Paradigm of Influence and Equity,* (Toplight, an imprint of McFarland and Company, Inc., 2021).

All Creatures Yearn to Be Free

All creatures, big and small, have this instinctive and innate yearning to be free. Freedom is an inborn gift from the universe and as humans we have this authentic longing to choose our own destiny. As the philosopher Jean Jacques Rousseau asserts (*Social Contract,* 1762), "Man is born free, but he is everywhere in chains."

Women's Struggle for Freedom and Equality

It has always intrigued me why women are treated as second-class citizens in the United States of America, the greatest bastion of freedom and democracy in the world. I was born and raised in Asia, where women were traditionally subservient to men. But in the Philippines, I grew up feeling valued, respected, and equal in status to my brothers and sisters. There was no question that, like my brothers, I would enter college and have my own career, even if I chose to get married. Even in the mid-1960s, women were doctors, engineers, architects, and governors and they assumed positions of power in both government and business. When I immigrated to this country, I assumed leadership positions in different departments of the State of Delaware and noticed the absence of females in decision-making and leadership positions. Later, as an executive coach, it baffled me as to why women leaders appear to either *abdicate* or *abuse* power. This blatant role perversion has and continues to confuse me. Why is there such a difficult and polarizing relationship between women and power?

The disastrous defeat of a highly experienced and trained woman, to an inexperienced, Machiavellian character of dubious integrity, dealt a castrating blow to women's fight for equality. Decades of struggle have not galvanized enough women—the vital many—to unite and claim power that could have resulted in enduring social change. This milestone event was the final blow that motivated me to do something of value to address this systemic and egregious problem.

On June 24, 2022, the United States Supreme Court voted to strike down Roe v. Wade, the 1973 landmark ruling that guaranteed women's constitutional right to abortion. It's ironic and disturbing that two of the justices who voted to overturn the ruling and deprived women of the right and freedom to choose—stripping away autonomy over their bodies—are alleged abusers (Kavanaugh and Thomas) of women themselves. These tectonic shifts appear to be simply the beginning of an organized backward movement, depriving women of equal rights and social justice. The *Make America Great Again* (MAGA) slogan is simply a call to action among right-wing conservative leaders to reclaim white male dominance in this country.

Power and Influence: The Missing Link

Power is the critical ingredient and the missing link in our struggle for equality and recognition. Although there have been giant steps towards gender parity, women still have major barriers to overcome to achieve a semblance of power and equality.

Our book, *Women Powered! A New Paradigm of Influence and Equity* was published by Toplight, an imprint of McFarland and Company, Inc., (2021). After some experience applying our new power model, I realized that this same framework could be applied as effectively in training male leaders, at the local, state, and federal levels.

We are at an existential crossroads in our country, which was exacerbated by the former incumbent's rule. He, with full support from his party, fomented conflict, division, and misinformation, and used lying as a way to govern. This style of leadership and governance stymied efforts to run the government smoothly, pass critical legislation to move the country forward, and resulted in the January 6, 2021, insurrection. As citizens of this country, we have a choice to make—strengthen our democracy or support the incipient autocracy that's rearing its spectral presence in our experiment in democracy.

Training to Be a Leader

In the United States, there is no traditional ritual, rite of passage or formalized training program for a president, his cabinet, members of Congress or any national leadership position that could enhance their abilities to effectively lead the country. The royals go through a mentoring program on how to be a king or a queen, learn formal etiquette and ways of behaving as a member of the monarchy. For example, Prince William has been a monarch-in-training since his youth, preparing for the day when he will ascend to the throne, after his father, Prince Charles' reign. According to the *Daily Mail* (www.dailymail.co.uk/news/article-1038961), "His lessons in the Art of Kingship will include working in different Whitehall departments to get a better idea of how government works, private instructions from constitutional experts, and briefings by privy councillors such as former prime minister Sir John Major." In some states, a short training is offered to members of the General Assembly, as in Delaware, New Jersey, New York, and California.

To be a Dalai Lama involves getting training from primary grades on, not only in academic subjects but also on the Buddhist philosophy. The 14th Dalai Lama's early training involved "The curriculum derived from the Nalanda Tradition, consisted of five major and five minor subjects. The major subjects included logic, fine arts, Sanskrit grammar and medicine, but the greatest emphasis was given to Buddhist philosophy . . ." (*Birth to Exile: The 14th Dalai Lama.* Retrieved on June 6, 2019, from www.dalailama.com/the-dalai-lama/biography-and-daily-life/birth-to-exile.)

The New Power Model: Character-Driven Leadership

The primary author completed intensive literature review on leadership and power, and through one-on-one interviews, various women in high-ranking government, administrative and business roles share their journeys, influences, and how they developed the key competencies and foundational traits to influence others. Based on these interviews, findings from a focus group, and the author's own experiences, this book proposes the application of a new power construct—*Character-Driven Leadership*—which rejects traditional Machiavellian concepts of power in favor of strategies such as honesty, trust, and competency through mentorship and training.

Character and Competencies: The Twin Towers

The two major components of the Character-Driven Leadership (CDL) are Character and Competencies:

Character and maturation-foundational traits: Required elements. Character refers to the moral and emotional characteristics and behavior distinctive to an individual. This key component represents the foundational traits that all aspiring leaders must possess to gain power and influence. They are required elements, not elective like the eight competencies presented in this model. The four elements that are portrayed in Figure 2 are foundational traits that require focus, attention, and practice for all men and women aspiring to be effective and powerful leaders. The four standard elements—*Know Thyself, Do It for Others, Do It for the Common Good, and Pursuit of the Truth*—form the framework for personal development and growth.

However, the approach to achieving growth and mastery in these areas can vary depending on individual choice. In other words, the "how" and techniques that leaders use to achieve the goal are non-prescriptive. Personal credibility, ethical and moral character, and principled-driven leadership are stronger attributes in gaining and sustaining the power equilibrium than simply professional competence.

Power, that's grounded in character and personal credibility, has a stronger staying power than one emanating from professional competence.

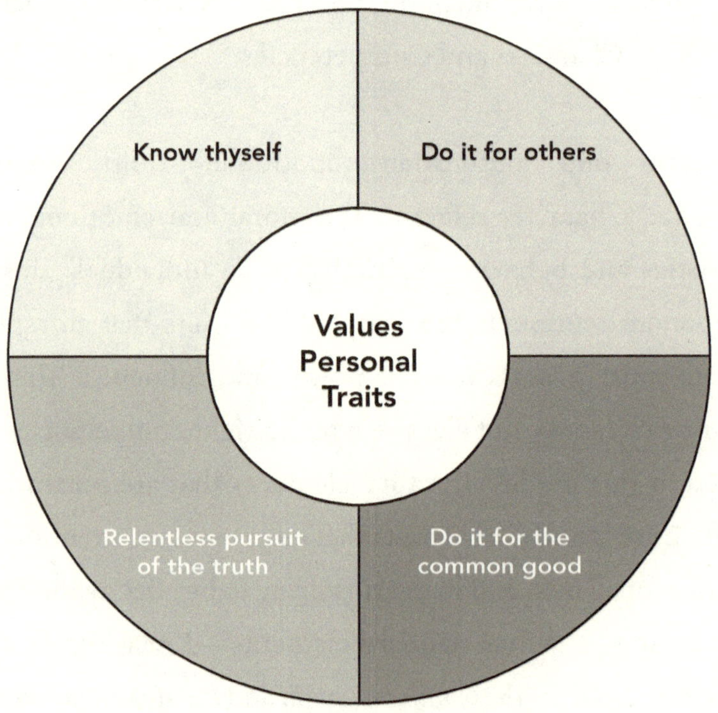

Figure 2: Character: Foundational Traits

CHARACTER: FOUNDATIONAL TRAITS

1. Know thyself
2. Do it for others
3. Do it for the common good
4. Relentless pursuit of the Truth

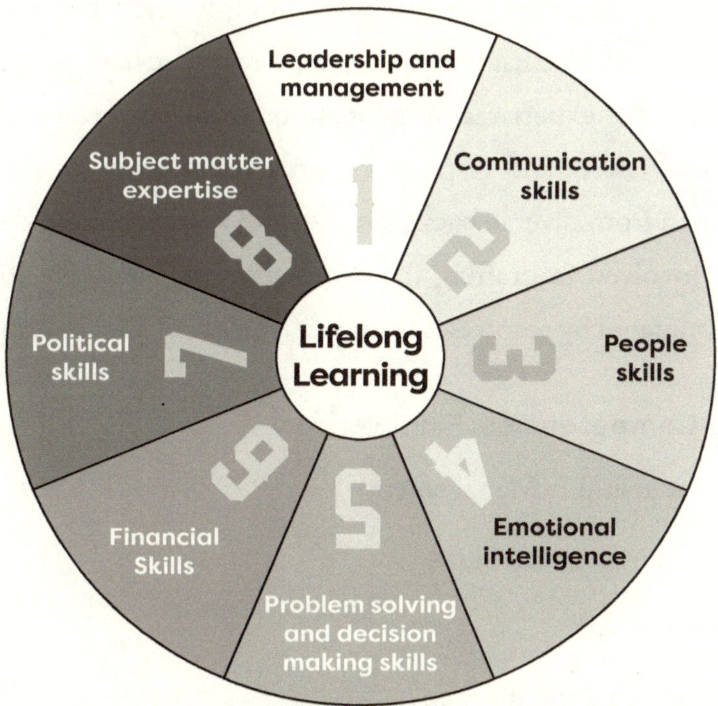

Figure 3: Eight Core Competencies

Competencies refer to the ability or capacity of individuals to do a job successfully and efficiently. To be competent, they must exhibit patterns of behavior that distinguish high performance when compared with those engaged in the same or comparable tasks or roles in a similar work environment. Professional competence alone is not sufficient to endow leaders with power; however, incompetent leaders have limited opportunities to fail and to suffer the loss of power. The eight core competencies presented in Figure 3 are suggested areas of proficiency for women and men who are attempting to learn the ways of the powerful. The list is based on a literature review of current research, the expert recommendations from powerful women we interviewed, and responses from a select group of women and men from diverse backgrounds, who comprised the design team involved in drafting the WomenPower Paradigm. It was also validated by responses from participants of a focus group.

Core Competencies: Final Version

1. Leadership & Management
2. Communication Skills
3. People Skills
4. Emotional Intelligence
5. Problem Solving & Decision-Making Skills
6. Financial Skills
7. Political Skills
8. Subject Matter Expertise

Systematic Process: Intentional, Deliberate, and Collective

As we have stated and stressed throughout the book, the only way to acquire and keep power is to be intentional and deliberate and to stay focused on the prize. The other critical ingredient in this journey of transformation and change is that it demands a collective effort. This individual and systems change requires an unrelenting focus on collaboration and support among all women and men.

As Christie Nolan, one of our key interviewees, noted, "If we plan to change longstanding patterns in our society around power, then we should shine a light on it and make intentional choices to practicing a new form of power—power that is collective, so we all have ownership in the results." Finally, she proclaimed, "If we are ever are going to make a change, we have to unpack and understand it all. We then use the information to make conscious choices about how we lead going forward. We are going to be more inclusive. We are going to create a more equitable society, organization, or board of directors, or whatever is right in front of us, with the intentional and deliberate choices that we make."

Intentional, deliberate, and systematic training of young women and women leaders might just be the tipping point that could change the power dynamics.

The Incandescent Joy at Finding Freedom

I have learned the most profound and insightful lessons about life and living from observing our pets and how they display their innermost feelings during emotionally charged moments. Our house rabbit Hershey, levitates into the open space, twirls around, and dances with youthful exuberance to express her unfettered joy and happiness for her newfound *freedom*. We rescued her from a pet sanctuary, where she was caged in for several years. Now, she is free to roam, to do her circular run, or just sit and stay cool and relaxed, knowing that she's free and safe. The instinctive and visceral feeling to be free is shared by all creatures. I can't wait to experience and feel the transforming energy of freedom and the affirming power of safety in an inclusive world of radical abundance, where there's enough of everything to go around and I can be free to just be me.

Parting Words: "To Live Past the End of Your Myth . . ."

When I was working as deputy director for a large department in the State of Delaware, I decided to retire early because I was searching for larger meaning and purpose and, I wanted to be certain that I didn't "overstay my welcome." My intent was to leave state employment while people still valued my abilities and contributions to the organization. It was the best decision

I ever made—it not only benefitted the organization but this early exit also promoted my personal and professional growth. As Canadian poet Anne Carson warned us, "To live past the end of your myth is a perilous thing." There are instances when political leaders, business leaders, CEOs, and other powerful figures "overstay their welcome" and fail to see the warning signs: the waning powers of their intellect, the misalignment between their skills and the organizational imperatives, and the needs and requirements of their customers and stakeholders, and other telltale signs of leadership degradation and decay. Still, they persist and they resist.

The temporal nature and sacredness of power dictate that we relinquish it when we're the wrong man or woman for the wrong time or when the greater good demands a new face and a new power model. We are called upon to move on and find our true north, rather than holding on to a tenuous state of inelegant decay. The brutal irony of this intransigent state is that we're the last ones to know when it's time to leave. Although, if we pause and try to listen to the whisper of that little voice within us, quietly screaming, "It's time to exit!" we might just overcome the inertia of fear and failure. Let's have the courage and the audacity to reflect and to move on, leave a lasting legacy, and transfer power to the next generation of trailblazers and leaders.

CHAPTER 13

What's the Purpose of Going to School?

ONE OF MY SONS got me thinking about this crucial but unresolved question when he made a remark concerning the value of pursuing further education to enhance his career. Just before this conversation, I happened to glance at a one-page ad promoting the financial advantages of going to graduate school. My readings show the predominance of the financial reason for engaging in public education and higher education.

What Other Experts Say

Arthur H. Camins posed the following question to his readers: "Should young people become educated to get prepared to enter the workforce, or should the purpose of education be focused more on social, academic, cultural and intellectual development so that students can grow up to be engaged citizens?" There are many different perspectives on this topic but Camins appears to have stated the problem in the clearest and most effective way. He pointed out that "Education should prepare young people for life, work, and citizenship." He concluded that it does not have to be an "either-or" proposition; it can be a multi-purpose perspective. Starting out with a clear mission statement is key to achieving the strategic goals, objectives, and outcomes set by leaders and stakeholders. Strategies, activities, and initiatives can then be systematically formulated to implement the mission and vision.

Contrast the elegant simplicity and clarity of mission advanced by Camins with the following purpose of education developed by the educational commission of a southeast Asian country: "All educational institutions shall inculcate patriotism and nationalism, foster love of humanity, respect for human rights, appreciation of the role of national heroes in the development of the country, teach the rights and duties of citizenship, strengthen ethical and spiritual values, develop moral character and personal discipline, encourage critical and creative thinking, broaden scientific and technological knowledge, and promote vocational efficiency." The mission is long, confusing, and not clearly stated. It would be difficult to implement this guideline for action because of its ambiguity, which can result in varying interpretations from decision makers and leaders.

Another model mission statement of the purpose of education is the summary presented in a paper by Professor Alan Reid, *Beyond Certainty: A Process for Thinking About Futures for Australian Education.* Below are the four purposes of the Australian Educational System:

1. Democratic Purpose. Schools are the main means society has to systematically develop young people as citizens who are able to play an active and constructive role in democratic life.

2. Economic Purpose. Schools make an important contribution to the Australian economy by preparing people for work in the many occupations that comprise the contemporary and future labour markets.

3. Individual Purpose. Schools provide opportunities for all children and young people to "acquire knowledge that takes them beyond their experience" (Young & Lambert, 2014, p. 10) and which enables them to lead rich, fulfilling, and productive lives. This purpose emphasizes that there does

not have to be a utilitarian purpose for education—it is significant in its own right.

4. Social and Cultural Purpose. Schools are an important means by which children and young people develop the understandings, skills, and dispositions necessary to play an active role with their fellow citizens in a diverse and multicultural civil society.

The mission statement above is clear, compelling, and multi-purpose. It does not have to be focused simply on a single priority, although realities confirm that the economic factor dominates Australian educational priorities.

My Personal Experience with Education

My curiosity about the purpose of education led me to another but parallel path of inquiry. I wondered why my students in the Philippines appear to value and enjoy learning, while my students in the United States appear to simply tolerate the experience and not really enjoy the process. I am aware that this is a gross generalization, but bear with me, and try to follow my thought pattern. Is it because education is an integral part of the Philippine value system and is validated by the actions and behaviors of all the key players—teachers, students, and parents? I wonder. This line of thinking led me to examine my own journey of discovery and transformation.

I didn't start enjoying learning until I was a freshman in high school. An English teacher named Mrs. Font turned me on to the study of World Literature, which opened a new, exciting, and unexplored world for me. My Economics teacher also motivated me to enjoy data and numbers and took a special interest in my ability to analyze, synthesize, and make meaning out of abstract concepts. I didn't know then that this stunning revelation, deploying both my left and right brain to full use, would be my secret to enjoying education and learning my entire adult life. When I entered the University of Santo Tomas, with a major in Sociology and English, I was completely hooked on learning. I flourished in the intellectual and creative university environment and totally loved and enjoyed learning. I found my bliss.

I entered the Ateneo Graduate School after completing my bachelor's degree, and majored in Sociology. The Ateneo University was an exclusive school for wealthy boys from prominent families, and it wasn't until the early 1960s that women were allowed to enroll in this institution. It was and still is considered one of the best, if not the best educational institution in the country. I learned and fell in love with doing quasi-experimental research, which I still use as an organizational consultant. My postgraduate work in the United States at Washington College and Nova Southeastern University sealed the deal—engaging in additional training and practice in research methods and techniques led me to a post-retirement career in organizational consulting.

Character and Competencies

My early education can be divided into two interconnected categories; one focused on *character development,* while the other centered on the development and mastery of *key competencies.* In school, we had courses in civics, appropriate conduct and behavior, and cultural values and mores that were integrated into every subject area. Basic subject matter areas included Reading, Writing, Mathematics, Social Studies, History (World History, Asian History, and Philippine History), English, Tagalog, and Science.

Education was formally administered by the Philippine educational system, but parents assumed a significant role in the education and socialization of their children.

I learned as much, if not more from my parents and siblings, while school simply provided me with the formal knowledge and information stream that I was informally imbibing within the family structure. My dad provided us with the latest magazine on world news, Great Books on philosophers and scientists, and Encyclopedia Britannica, more updated than the collections at the local school libraries. My dad was a journalist, and his colleagues frequently gathered at our house for an evening of conversation. I was a young kid then, and so curious about what adults were talking about. I would pull up my little chair and insert myself in between the adults' chairs. I just listened, didn't speak a peep, but it brought my world bite-sized learning about the universe around me and exciting morsels of information that were new and magical to me. We now call this type of learning micro-learning, snippets of interesting and new information and knowledge, much like factual tweets. I was mesmerized! I was like a sponge, absorbing all this pristine and vibrant knowledge and information, with no one censoring my free-flowing curiosity.

I learned through experience how to lead and manage effectively by observing the way my mother managed and supervised the household staff, facilitated the League of Women's Voter's meetings, and the way she interacted with elected officials when advocating for a social justice issue that she cared about. I also learned honesty, integrity, and how to wield power effectively and ethically by observing my father's interactions with his office staff, the elected officials who tried to bribe and to silence him, and how to stand up to power. It was not uncommon for my dad to take my siblings and me to his office or to special meetings with him. On one special occasion, he took me to an informal meeting with the president of the Philippines. I was barely five years old and didn't appreciate the significant impact of this momentous experience. I carried on a casual conversation with President Ramon Magsaysay, the 7th president of the Philippines. He treated me with respect and kindness, actively listened to what I was saying, and promptly answered the simple questions that I asked. He was a magnanimous man, a servant leader, who truly cared for the common people and his beloved country.

I also learned how to appreciate the arts, music, and the world of entertainment through frequent trips to museums and art exhibits; performances by internationally renowned symphony orchestras; ballet performances; and operas, like Carmen (Bizet), La Boheme and Tosca (Puccini) and Aida (Verdi). I also attended concerts by popular artists like Paul Anka and Harry Belafonte. However, I didn't realize until later in life that not all people had a privileged childhood like mine. I am so grateful to my parents and to the Universe for granting me this favored and legendary childhood. I appreciated it then and I am even more appreciative of it now that I am an older adult.

No wonder I love learning and have pursued this passion all my life. My parents, my early childhood education, my later experiences in higher education, magnificent life opportunities, and a privileged life shaped and enhanced my passion for knowledge and learning.

Purpose Is Ever Changing: Alignment with Social, Economic, Cultural, and Technological Realities

It's important to remember that the key purpose of education is ever-changing and will remain constant only for a targeted period of time. It will change depending on the needs and requirements of students and teachers, leaders and stakeholders, and the political, economic, socio-cultural, and technological factors (PEST) affecting the entire country. Leaders and decision makers must do an environmental scan of the strengths, weaknesses, opportunities, and threats PEST posed by the factors listed above. It's a complex issue that requires a complex and systemic solution. Kim Jones, CEO of Curriki outlined the many goals of education that have evolved through decades of transformation and change. They are:

- To prepare children for citizenship
- To cultivate a skilled workforce
- To teach literacy
- To help students become critical thinkers
- To help students compete in a global marketplace

Education need not have a single purpose. As was noted by Camins, "Education should prepare young people for life, work, and citizenship." The manner in which we deliver education through highly trained educators, and how we measure outcomes must also be aligned to match the purposes of education. Hence, the need for continuous improvement through systemwide strategic planning and implementation. The process does not end here. It's a continuous and never-ending process of improvement, alignment, planning, and action.

CHAPTER 14

Parenting 3.0

How to Build a Better Relationship with Your Adult Children

"WHAT HAVE I done to my kids," I exclaimed with mixed trepidation and horror, when my boys came home from college during the holiday break. These characters looked different from the clean-shaven, private school-educated boys that I knew—who were just home not so many months ago. One waltzed in with an earring in one ear and long hair, while the other sported longer hair and a tattoo on one of his ankles. What blasphemy is this? What happened to the dress shirt, with necktie neatly resting underneath the collar, and the well-groomed schoolboy haircut? I was too stunned to move and talk, so I simply stared at this apparition—much like a deer blinded and frozen by headlights of an oncoming car. My first reaction was to blame myself; I am the parent and it's my job to guide and shape the behavior of these young adults. I didn't realize then that this was actually a fairly benign occurrence. The boys were simply trying to define their emerging identities, making choices and decisions, without any influence or intervention from me, the parent. This was part and parcel of what I call *Parenting 2.0,* when the young adults leave the home front for college, in pursuit of independence, freedom, and a life of their choosing.

Parenting 1.0 was actually a breeze, when the boys were children, and all I had to contend with were the terrible twos, tantrums, toilet training, and feeding dependent children. They didn't start to rebel until age thirteen, and it was comparatively a bearable and not terribly unpleasant phase. They didn't have the competencies as yet to launch a well-formed assault on rational arguments since their pre-frontal cortex was still developing. And they also lacked the solid experience and practice to mount a winning argument.

Parenting: A Lifetime Job

Parenting has been and continues to be the most challenging job I will ever have. The roles and responsibilities never stay the same—they are always in a state of transition and change. It has baffled me as to why there is no formal training offered in a standardized curriculum (maybe in high school), where young women and men get knowledge training and practical instructions on the roles and responsibilities of parenting. How we raise our children affects the quality of life of future generations and the well-being of the entire country.

I learned how to be a good mother by modeling my behavior after my mom and dad, who happened to be the best parents. I also credit Dr. Benjamin Spock whose seminal book, *Baby and Child Care* (1968, Revised Edition) became the primer for millions of parents. He made me feel more confident and self-reliant with comments like mothers "know more than they think," and advising us to focus on the needs of the child. He also reminded us to be flexible and to treat the child as a unique individual, which was a radical approach at that period in time. *Parenting 1.0* was primarily influenced by the parenting I received from my own parents and from reading Dr. Spock's new approach to child rearing.

Parenting 2.0 was less traumatic and challenging, except financially, because both boys were in college. After college, the oldest decided to fly away and start his own career. The younger one came back home for a short stop, until he was able to get a steady job and save to buy his house. While they were in college, I was fully engaged in promoting my career, getting additional degrees, and traveling around the world. Nothing bothered me because I was enjoying life and the freedom to shape the life of my choice.

Parenting 3.0, being a mother to adult children (say, from 30 years old and older), is more of a tricky proposition. Now, they have their own families, careers, and new sets of roles and responsibilities. They're autonomous and equal to you. They truly have very little need for you or your guidance, not unless they ask you for feedback. It's during this transition that parents appear to have greater need for support, assistance, and guidance from adult children. When parents enter old age (say, 70 +), a majority have less physical endurance and cognitive stamina, and are less able to do most of the chores that they used to perform independently. Some suffer from major physical and mental illness, such as cancer, heart problems, and dementia. The parent has now become the child—a role reversal that seems to happen gradually, then suddenly, old age and dependency set in. Psychologists refer to this swift decline in cognitive functioning and verbal skills as a *terminal drop,* which typically happens 1–5 years before death. This is the hardest phase of the parenting journey—when parents are in denial and adult children have to contend with the inevitable decline, confusion, and conflict. Put a pin on that thought and we'll revisit the resolution section towards the end of this chapter. Meaningful change requires a complete reset of the relationship between older parents and adult children.

Cultural Prism: A Drawback for Immigrant Parents

Culture consists of beliefs, values, behaviors, and material objects that constitute a people's way of life (Macionis, 2013). It represents a shared way of life that provides us with messages that shape our beliefs, perceptions, values, and judgments about who we are, how we relate to others, and how we behave within a society. It is a powerful element that regulates order in society, moderates individual behavior, and oftentimes is manifested in automatic and unconscious ways. There were occasions when I got in trouble with my American friends because I was operating from the Filipino cultural cue in an American setting. For example, when I was in college and in graduate school, I always aimed to do my level best, not because I was competing with my classmates, but because I was raised in a culture that valued excellence, education, and self-growth. The motivator is internal, not the external reward of being number one or being the winner in the competition to get the best grade. To Americans, this is unreal; I am a fake. In another instance, I got in trouble when I lavished love, attention, and time on an extended member of my family. The American relative accused me of competing with her for the child's love and attention. It was farthest from the truth. I was simply operating from my old cultural code, reflexively, totally unaware that this was labelled competition in the American setting.

The early parenting years were relatively uneventful because I had a lot of control and influence on the basic rules of the game—the children were young, immature, and completely dependent on me. Confusion, disagreements, and minor conflicts emerged during later years, when the boys became young adults. They were operating from the American playbook, while I was still marginally following both American and Filipino cultural cues. Maybe I was guided by American norms and mores 70 percent of the time, while operating on the Filipino ways of behaving 30 percent of the time. To top it all, I was unaware of these internal cultural dynamics, all manifested in my behavior. Sometimes, acquaintances would comment that "You are now in America, so you should behave like an American." It definitely is easier said than done. It's impossible to tease out what's American and what's Filipino in my parenting repertoire. The Filipino component is buried deep in the subterranean level of the iceberg, while the American dimension shines right on the tip. All along, I thought I was a thoroughly Americanized parent.

Now that I am an older American, I have been encountering areas of resistance that I have not experienced before. After much reflection and self-flagellation, I realize that my mental model of my parenting skills has remained stagnant since I was in my 50s. Now that I am at the yawning abyss of old age, I still operate with my antiquated parenting strategies, and have not adapted to the changing needs and requirements of my older, more mature, and autonomous adult children. I need to polish and update my parenting competencies to complement their needs. Now, are you beginning to appreciate the quandary that an immigrant parent faces, on top of the challenges posed by the complexity and the forever-nature of the parenting role?

Ask Sabrina: My Objective Alter-Ego

When I am confronted with a confusing and life-altering problem, I often consult with my alter-ego, my avatar in a parallel universe, Sabrina. She is cool, optimistic, and uses her whole brain to break tasks into mini-goals to make them easier to tackle. She is a risk-taker and uses her heart and her mind to transform obstacles into fuel. I had a session with her last month to brainstorm on how to improve my relationship with my adult children, now that they are independent, fully-functioning adults. I also asked her for pointers on how to evolve into the *new me*—the really *old-old me,* that is, when the time comes that I am not able to take care of my daily needs anymore.

Suggestions for Improvement

Here is Sabrina's advice on how to forge a stronger, steady, and loving relationship with my adult children during this parenting phase in my life, which might also be useful for some of you:

1. **Draft a plan of action and discuss roles and responsibilities:** Now that you are nearing the period where your adult kids are mature, self-sufficient, and capable, while you're trekking down the opposite direction, you might need to have a family discussion on your fluid and changing roles, responsibilities, and needs. You, as the aging parent, need to adjust to the new dynamics, and clarify your needs and expectations about critical topics, while you have the time and the mental ability to do so. Below are examples of topics that require discussion and resolution:
    - Where would you want to live? Do you prefer staying home, moving closer to one of the kids, or another living arrangement?
    - When do you want to move? It might be wise to make the change while you're still physically, mentally, and emotionally able to make clear and sensible decisions.
    - How much money do you have in savings, investments, pensions, and other sources? Are they enough to pay for this change in lifestyle?
    - Do you have a will; a living will?
    - Can you drive safely? If not, how are you going to move around and handle basic transactions, like going to the supermarket, the bank, doctors, and other daily activities?

2. **Have open, honest, and respectful communication:** Communication is a prerequisite for any relationship. You might not always agree, but common ground is impossible without continuing discussion, exchange of ideas, and resolution.

3. **Equal Adults:** As an older parent, you have to change perspective and treat your older children as adults and autonomous individuals worthy of respect.

4. **Hold off on feedback, unless asked:** Your wisdom from years of experience and learning is overflowing and you need to release it somehow. Stop the flow, barricade the gates, and refrain from releasing your wisdom, unless you're asked.

5. **Adapt style of parenting with the phase that you're in:** When the kids were young and dependent, you exercised complete control over their lives, like a queen or king, lording over her kingdom, or a boss, managing employees. Now that they are equal in wisdom and knowledge, and might even have surpassed your abilities, you're there only to listen, react, and validate their accomplishments with your affirmations and praise. If you're lucky, they might consult you and ask for your opinion on matters of importance.

6. **Be resilient, flexible, and open to constructive feedback:** When I became a mother, I started to truly grow up and to

shift focus from self to others. When you lift others up, you begin to grow and practice the virtues of patience, tenacity, resilience, and love. I tried to use these learned skills to navigate the treacherous and oftentimes unpredictable waters of old age. Sometimes I succeed, but there are many times when I fail. Resilience is the name of the game.

7. **Relationship is grounded in love and respect:** When there's disagreement and breakdown in communication, pause and simply listen. You're coming from two generations with different values and behaviors that can cause a deep chasm in relationship. Factor in the cultural gap when your parents are immigrants from another country, and the meeting of minds gets more challenging. Remember that you are the parent, who is supposed to model the desired behavior. Whatever you do has to come from a place of love and respect for each other. As an adult child, be patient and accommodating if your parent has diminished cognitive, physical, and emotional capabilities. Remember, this is the final journey that both of you have to take. You would like to remember this time with sheer joy, compassion, and enduring love. The ability to plow through pain and suffering together, and survive loving each other more, is a gift from the universe available to all.

CHAPTER 15

Widowhood

One Is the Loneliest Number

"WIDOWS ARE THE FORGOTTEN demographics," noted a report by Hamermesh, Myck, and Oczkowska (*The Challenging Plight of Widows,* May 19, 2021), published on the website of IZA World of Labor. The article noted that in Western countries, widows, ages 70+, constitute about half of that age group, and 11 percent of all adult women. Although widows are faced with enormous challenges in many areas of their lives, and despite their significant number, few social scientists have engaged in doing research on this group of older adults.

Data on Widows

In the United States, widowhood among older Americans (adults aged 75 and up) is equally prevalent and mirrors the data from the report by IZA World of Labor. There are currently 54.2 percent of widowed women in this age cohort, compared with 19.5 percent of widowed men, as displayed in the table below:

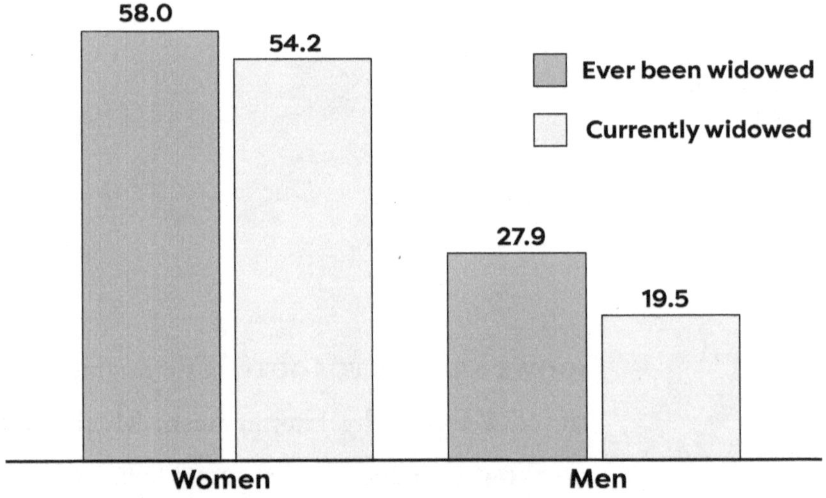

Source: U.S. Census Bureau, Survey of Income and Program Participation, 2014 Panel, Wave 1.

Figure 4: Widowhood Among US Adults Ages 75 and Up

Gurrentz and Yeris Mayol-Garcia, (*Marriage, Divorce, Widowhood Remain Prevalent Among Older Populations,* April 22, 2021).

Depression and Other Problems Facing Widows

Widowhood is a life disruption that many older Americans face. A recent study in the *American Journal of Geriatric Psychiatry* found that 27 percent of older adults assessed by service providers met the criteria for a diagnosis of major depression (Thomas Richardson, et al). Data released by Mental Health America *(Depression in Older Adults: More Facts)* indicated that one-third of widows/widowers meet the criteria for clinical depression during the first month after the death of their spouse, and half remain depressed after one year. In addition to loneliness and depression, widows face economic, social, and sometimes cultural barriers. Women experience financial strain because their husbands typically earned higher incomes. Transitions and adaptations in social relationships exacerbate widows' sense of self since their identity is frequently tied to their husbands' social status. Cultural norms often favor couples over singles and widows have to redefine their social role in a society where there are no clear-cut definitions of where they belong. Before the prohibition of the practice of suttee in India, widows were encouraged to self-immolate by sitting on the deceased husband's funeral pyre. Although not widely practiced, it was supposed to symbolize a wife's ideal devotion to her husband. In Zimbabwe, *(Widows Deprived of Property Rights, Human Rights Watch,* January 24, 2017) widows are deprived of their homes, land, and other properties by their in-laws, according to a report released in 2017 by the Human Rights Watch *(You Will Get Nothing: Violations of Property and Inheritance Rights of Widows in Zimbabwe,* 2017). In America, widows are at least spared these devastating cultural anomalies.

Living Alone

According to an article by Daniel B. Kaplan and Barbara J. Berkman *(Older Adults Living Alone,* March 2021), "In the US, about 28 percent (14.7 million) of community-dwelling older adults live alone, which is 21 percent of older men and 34 percent of older women. The percentage of people living alone increases with age (ie., among women ≥ 75 years, about 44 percent live alone)." Solo living further exacerbates the feelings of loneliness and isolation felt by widowed older adults.

In a study of older adults (60+) in 130 countries in the Asia-Pacific, sub-Saharan Africa, and the Middle East-North Africa regions, Jacob Ausubel of the Pew Research Center noted that only 16 percent of older adults live alone. Nearly 4 in 10 older adults (38 percent) live in an extended family household, where they reside with relatives, such as grandchildren, adult children and their spouses, nephews and nieces. This living arrangement affords older people the care and support of family members and provides them with opportunities for strong connections and relationship-building.

I have been a widow since I was thirty-six years old and have managed to transition to a happier, more satisfying life after four decades of adjustment, trial, and experimentation.

When I was first widowed and when my sons left home for college, I often turned to my therapeutic habit of talking to the wall to adapt to a strange new world. It's my way of making an instant connection with "someone" other than myself. When you live alone, you neutralize the silence, sometimes the loneliness, by carrying on a two-way conversation with someone willing to listen.

The wall inspires me to look within myself whenever I have a problem that needs a solution, or when I am deliriously happy and I just have to share my joy with someone. Wally, the wall is always there to listen. My phantom friend is always available, silent, obedient, and affable. He never disagrees or complains, never ever raises his voice or answers back. Like a potted plant, he always stands ready and able, to just simply observe and not fracture the silence. Wally is just always there. Present. Dependable. As an individual living alone, I manage to stay happy and connected by crafting coping mechanisms like my friendship with Wally. I know he isn't real but he helps me survive and navigate my solo life more smoothly.

I also used other typical coping tools, such as keeping a journal, taking long walks in the woods, doing meditation, and connecting with family and friends. My work became the centerpiece of my life after my sons left, because it afforded me the opportunity to help employees and clients and it gave me a whole new powerful purpose in life.

In my book *SoloPower: How to Harness the Secret Energy of Living Alone* (2014), I did a study on the happiness levels of people in this country who live alone and factors that make them happy or unhappy. The findings of the survey indicated that a clear majority of individuals who live alone are either "Happy" (41 percent) or "Very Happy" (23 percent) most of the time, which appears to be contrary to common perceptions. The top five reasons that made individuals who live alone happy or unhappy based on all three methods—the online survey, focus groups, and case studies—are summarized below:

What makes people who live alone happy?

- Relationship with children, grandchildren, family, friends, and God
- Self-knowledge, self-reliance, and ability to control their lives
- Engaging in meaningful activities that give purpose to their lives: e.g., contributing to the lives of others
- Staying healthy
- Having a positive attitude

What makes people who live alone unhappy?

- Loneliness and absence of intimacy
- Inability to share the joys and sorrows of their lives
- Ill health
- Making challenging decisions without feedback from a partner
- Financial concerns

How to Improve the Quality of Life for Widows and Widowers

There's great need for widows and other older adults who live alone to become more involved in their community, and leaders and practitioners to raise awareness on the importance of connections and relationships to minimize loneliness and social isolation. There are many activities at senior centers that can alleviate the isolation and loneliness experienced by most older adults. For example, at a local senior center in the city where I live, there are social, recreational, and educational activities, which range from computer tutoring, dance lessons, language lessons, gardening, and trips around the country and abroad. The center offers Meals on Wheels, an employment program, adult day services, caregiver resource center, an early memory loss program, and a long list of additional services to live a fuller and more engaging life.

Coordination and delivery of services for patients living alone is challenging at best and could be mitigated by those involved in healthcare delivery. The *Merck Manual for Professionals* suggests that "Physicians should ensure that home care is available and recommend additional services, as appropriate. A passive or individually activated emergency response device may reassure patients that help can be obtained if needed. Since the onset of the COVID-19 pandemic, many community-based mental health and social care providers have increased capacity for technology-enabled outreach and service." In addition to taking these recommended steps, it would benefit this population (and all patients) if physicians would spend quality time listening to patients and appropriately using the patient interview and assessment as an effective diagnostic tool, instead of simply processing the patient and referring her to another specialist. Primary care physicians should take responsibility for the effective coordination and delivery of healthcare to their patients.

At the policy and more strategic level, we need live and current data about this demographic cohort that will allow decision makers and leaders to make informed decisions on the needs and requirements of this group. Legislation, policies, and projects, where considerable amount of dollars are spent, should be based on empirical data and just-in-time information and knowledge.

Family, friends, and neighbors can alleviate the loneliness, social isolation, and need for support experienced by widows through simple acts of kindness and concern. Invite your mom and dad to share a Sunday meal with you and your family; call, text or FaceTime with them and check on their physical and emotional health; assist them in doing tasks they are unable to do because of mobility and balance issues. Sometimes, older widows need assistance getting to appointments, attending to their personal hygiene, or simply taking medications. There are a million and one things that family, friends, and neighbors can do to help them not feel helpless or discouraged, to continue to live independent lives (if that's their choice), and to improve the quality of life for this forgotten population. Start now, and continue advocating for vital members of our family and community, who not so long ago dedicated their lives so that we may survive and flourish.

CHAPTER 16

Polarization, Normlessness, and American Values

WHAT ARE VALUES and why are they important? Values refer to intangible qualities or beliefs considered good, right, and desirable by a given society and are manifested in the behavior of individuals. They are deeply embedded in a society's culture and become automatic and reflexive as they become integrated into individuals' subconscious minds. For example, American values include equality, individualism, competition, action, work orientation, and materialism to name a critical few.

I suspect that the polarization and normlessness that we are experiencing in our nation right now could be linked to our values of individualism and competition. Values form and shape the collective cultural make-up of our institutions and ultimately the social fabric of the American society. In the pages that follow, I will share with you my perspective on the possible correlation between our values and the polarization that we are faced with at this moment in our nation's history.

Individualism vs. a Collectivist Culture

Americans firmly believe that every person is unique, self-sufficient, and independent. The rights of individuals to choose are critically important and are considered distinct and separate from families, communities, and society in general. Americans do not like to think of themselves as dependent on others; they prefer to shape their own destinies and choose their preferred pathways in life. This fierce sense of individualism came in full spectacle during the recent COVID-19 pandemic, where a sizeable number of Americans refused to comply with mandatory vaccination, masking, and other preventive measures to minimize the spread of the virus. We are now in year-four, and we're still confounded by the surging numbers of COVID-19 cases and long-haul COVID cases. Individualism, carried to extremes, has invaded the health landscape of our lives.

Author and educator Kendra Cherry noted that "Collectivist Cultures emphasize the needs and goals of the group as a whole over the needs and desires of each individual. In such cultures, relationships with other members of the group and the *interconnectedness between* people play a central role in each person's identity." In our complex and ever-changing society, systemic and intractable problems cannot be solved by a single individual; it requires the effort and brainpower of a collective representing diverse disciplines and perspectives. Collaboration, creativity, and the ability to work seamlessly as a team are fundamental requirements to achieving our collective goals. The global problems confronting the world today, such as poverty and food insecurity, ecological disaster, unemployment, homelessness, and endemic social injustice plaguing every continent are beyond the span of control and influence of discrete individuals and individual nations.

Competition vs. Collaboration

A pervasive American value that permeates every area of American life is competition. Its ubiquitous presence can be seen in sports, in business, in schools, in employment, and in every American institution—social, economic, political, even religious institutions. It plays out even among families and friends. It is celebrated as a virtue and as a cherished value that's imparted to young men at an early age. Americans believe that this quintessential value brings out the best in Americans—a powerful motivator for creativity, innovation, and economic success.

Is healthy competition beneficial, that is, if we keep everything in perspective? Or is competition inherently a destructive and pernicious practice? In the competition equation, when someone succeeds, the other fails. Why do we have to have winners and losers? Why can't we all be winners? Reflect on this simple but profound reality—the collective or individual standard for excellence can be the internal barometer for success. I can "compete" with myself. Collectively, our American society can have well-defined standards of excellence for success, whether we aim for success in sports, in business, in the workplace or in any other endeavor. Besides, isn't there enough of everything to go around (del Tufo, *Behind the Golden Door,* 2017).

Valuing competition as a powerful, animating force towards achieving excellence, Americans have crafted free enterprise to complement this value and to demonstrate its effectiveness in realizing individual and collective affluence—the American dream.

G. William Domhoff presented convincing evidence in his classic book entitled *Who Rules America? Power, Politics and Social Change* (2005) that power in America is dominated by a fixed group of privileged people and corporations. Outlined below are his startling conclusions on the rule by a power elite and their control of wealth in this country, which dominates both the America economy and government (del Tufo, *Behind the Golden Door,* 2017).

- "The rich" coalesce into a social upper class that has developed institutions by which the children of its members are socialized into an upper class worldview, and newly wealthy people are assimilated.
- Members of this upper class control corporations, which have been the primary mechanisms for generating and holding wealth in the United States for upwards of 150 years now.
- There exists a network of nonprofit organizations through which members of the upper class and hired corporate leaders not yet in the upper class shape policy debates in the United States.
- Members of the upper class, with the help of their high-level employees in profit and nonprofit institutions, are able to dominate the federal government in Washington.
- The rich, and corporate leaders, nonetheless claim to be relatively powerless.
- Working people have less power than in many other democratic countries.

Domhoff offered a well-thought-out analysis and review of the interwoven linkages and vested interests of the American upper class, and the corporate and political elements of this society. The ordinary citizen is relatively powerless in the face of the concentrated power wielded by this singular entity. Is there truly open competition and free enterprise in this country, when power and the economic engine is controlled by a power elite?

Certainly, competition cannot be the only animating force that drives us towards excellence. Ruthless competition does not appear to benefit the common good since only a small group of individuals benefit from it. How about looking into the beneficial aspects of cooperation and support as a driving force for success? Can it replace competition as the new lifeblood of American society? We preach teamwork, cooperation, and partnership in the workplace, in schools, in sports, and practically everywhere, but our actions demonstrate the opposite. There's lack of alignment between what we say and what we do. Is the American Dream simply an unreachable dream for most of us?

Individualism and Normlessness

Emile Durkheim, the "father of Sociology," introduced the current concept of *anomie* in his seminal book *The Division of Labor in Society* (1893). He believed that in modern society, there's a fair degree of agreement on norms and values that regulate accepted behavior in society. Acceptance and compliance are fairly stable when societal change is minimal. However, during times of rapid social change, (e.g., revolution, pandemic, economic depression), when norms, values, and ways of behaving are in transition, people start to doubt and become unsure of accepted ways of behaving. It's at this critical time that *anomie* or normlessness happens—the blurring and eventual breakdown of norms that regulate individual and collective standards of behavior. Durkheim noted that that normlessness happens more often in societies where individualism predominates because they lack the social solidarity that acts as a protective shield by minimizing the effects of external threats on individuals. I thought that this approach could be useful to decision makers and leaders as they reflect on the *root causes* of normlessness and polarization in our country today.

Robert Merton *(Social Structure of Anomie,* 1938) applied Durkheim's theory to the United Stated and "argued that *anomie* is not simply about unregulated goals, but a broken relationship between cultural goals and legitimate means of accessing them." He noted that Americans are socialized to believe that possibilities for success are limitless, no matter what barriers you're facing. He also pointed out that there's a *misalignment between cultural goals and legitimate access* of achieving them. When there's a mismatch, then deviance occurs and some elements of the population resort to illegitimate means to achieve societal goals. This could explain why during this current time, there's rampant crime and violence in our country. According to a report *(Is the Criminal Justice System Working?)* published by USA Facts on Crime and Justice, murders increased by 29.4 percent between 2019 and 2020, while burglaries decreased by 7.4 percent. The report on *Violent Crimes in America* published by the Statista Research Department (September 30, 2021), noted that the total number of violent crimes in America is 1.3 million, which is 398.5 per 100,000 inhabitants. Violent crimes are very much alive in America. The report indicated that "In the United States, violent crimes are defined as incidents involving force or the threat of force. The main offences reported under violent crime are murder and non-negligent manslaughter, rape and sexual assault, robbery, and aggravated assault." Maybe, leaders and decision-makers from governmental entities, corporations, and nonprofits can commission studies looking at the root causes of social problems in this country and involve sociologists, criminologists, and experts from other disciplines before pouring millions of dollars into addressing them.

The Enemy Is Us

There is a reflexive tendency among humans to first look externally for the problem and cast the blame on others. Since 9/11, our country has been laser-focused in eliminating the threat from Muslim countries that culminated in the death of Osama Bin Ladin and more recently the assassination of the al Qaeda leader Ayman al-Zawahiri in a drone strike. We are becoming more aware of the existential threats posed by the Russians, the Chinese, the North Koreans, and the Iranians. Sometimes, we fail to appreciate the danger from within, as in the spectacle of the January 6, 2021, insurrection. Even after listening to the disturbing findings uncovered by the January 6 House Select Committee, the American public appears unfazed by this attack on our democracy, and the former president's efforts to overturn the results of the 2020 presidential election and prevent the transfer of power.

The public remains polarized, society appears to be separating at the seams, and there's a profound lack of trust in our leaders, governments, and institutions. There's normalization of deviance, criminal behavior among the powerful, and lowering of standards. What happened to our cherished values of honesty, integrity, national pride, and love of country? Is it a question of character and substance? What happened to the American National Character? And yet, some of our values are carried to extremes, like individualism and competition. It's a confounding national calamity. We all need to pause and reflect on our role in this equation, and how our individual and collective values and institutions have led us to this precipice.

Robert Bellah (*The Good Society,* 1991) and his colleagues argued that we, as Americans, must own the social problems confronting us right now, and be accountable for the failures of our institutions and the devastating outcomes. We have to take the lead in this transformation by creating a more effective and morally conscious society. The authors reminded us that "autonomy, valuable as it is in itself, is only one virtue among others and that without such virtues as responsibility and care, which can be exercised only through institutions, [autonomy becomes] an empty form without substance."

Finally, President John F. Kennedy cautioned us that "There are risks and costs to action. But they are far less than the long-range risks of comfortable inaction."

CHAPTER 17

A Balanced Life

Planning for Wellness, Well-Being, and Happiness for Older Adults

PLANNING IS IMPORTANT IN our daily lives, and assumes greater importance during critical life transitions, such as retirement and moving into old age—where independence and control over your lives are diminishing. Planning gives you a roadmap to get to your goals, a clear perspective on priorities, and a way to stay on track despite the constant changes inherent in life. It also allows you to monitor and adjust to the changes, which sometimes are beyond your control. Life is unpredictable, and a plan provides you with a protective armor against life's challenges, much like a parachute that slows down your descent and allows you to drift gracefully and safely to the ground.

One of the services I provide as an organizational consultant is facilitating a strategic planning session, where employees and their leaders take time out from their daily routine and engage in defining goals and priorities for their organization. The exercise involves defining the mission, vision, objectives, and goals for their organization. I typically use the Balanced Scorecard (BSC) method, which I think is superior to the garden-variety type of strategic planning because it looks at outcomes and budgets as part of the overall picture. It is both an effective planning and measurement tool.

In the pages that follow, I will share with you two planning models to help you map out the coming decades of your life. The first is more comprehensive and detailed than the other; the second model is fairly simple, direct, and not as time-consuming.

Model 1: A Balanced Scorecard for Life—The Process

The simplest way to show you how to do this model is to map out a structured process, list the steps in sequential order, and identify the eight different dimensions of wellness and well-being that you are trying to achieve.

PAPAR is the acronym for the Balanced Scorecard for Life process and it stands for the following:

P= Purpose and Priorities

A= Alignment and Balance

P= Problem-Solve

A= Act and Implement

R= Review and Redo

Step 1: Purpose & Priorities

The first step in the process is to identify your mission or purpose in life, which might change drastically as you transition from full-time work to maybe, semi-retirement or full retirement from paid employment. Your personal mission and vision provide guidance and direction in this new life status. It's much like a directional compass that guides you as you discover your new purpose and establish priorities during this time in your life. The primacy of the *Occupational Dimension* (Figure 5) would likely diminish as you slide into a different lifestyle and move out of the competitive world of work. At age 60, I focused more on the *Social, Emotional, and Intellectual Dimensions* of life. On the next page are sample personal mission statements that guided me as I navigated the untested waters of retirement and elderhood:

- Mission 1: To love and cherish my family and friends (Social & Emotional)
- Mission 2: To be of service to others and be a positive force in my community (Social & Spiritual)
- Mission 3: To study and learn in greater depth topics of your choice and engage in lifelong learning (Intellectual)

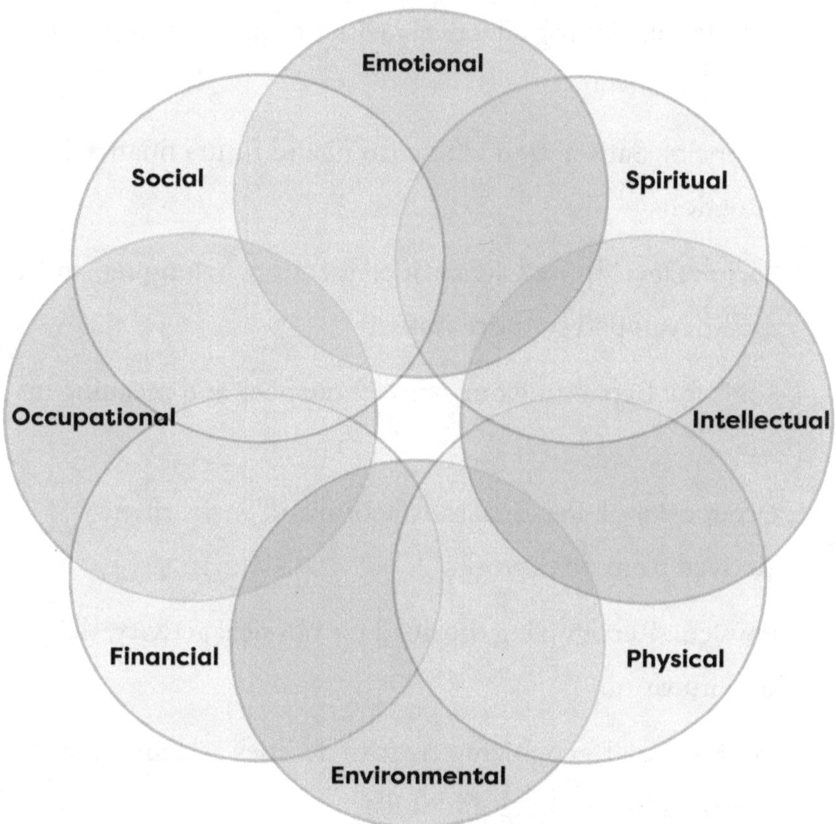

Figure 5: Eight Dimensions of Wellness and Well-Being—Planning Wheel for Individuals 60 Years and Older.
Substance Abuse & Mental Health Services Administration Model

Eight Dimensions of Wellness and Well-Being

The dimensions outlined below are based on Substance Abuse and Mental Health Services Administration's (SAMHSA) model and are designed to maximize individuals' overall health and quality of life (https://store.samhsa.gov/sites/default/files/d7/priv/sma16-4953.pdf).

1. Emotional: Coping effectively with life and creating satisfying relationships
2. Financial: Satisfaction with current and future financial situations
3. Social: Developing a sense of connection, belonging, and a well-developed support system
4. Spiritual: Expanding our sense of purpose and meaning in life
5. Occupational: Personal satisfaction and enrichment derived from one's work
6. Physical: Recognizing the need for physical activity, sleep, and nutrition
7. Intellectual: Recognizing creative abilities and finding ways to expand knowledge and skills
8. Environmental: Good health by occupying pleasant, stimulating environments that support well-being

Step 2: Alignment & Balance

Let me point out that alignment between your life mission and your new priorities in the eight Dimensions of Wellness and Well-Being is not always easy to achieve, and close to perfect balance is at best an ideal goal. Your task is to simply align your mission with your new priorities as close as you can. You might choose to focus your energies on those vital few dimensions and neglect ones that are not critical to your wellness and well-being during this evolving transition phase. For example, my number one priority is to spend quality time with my family and friends, so I might have less discretionary time to focus and nurture the Occupational and Financial dimensions. I am still working part-time, but I stopped marketing my services and cut down the number of clients in my practice. As long as it is your conscious choice and you feel reasonably content with it, then you'll be fine.

Step 3: Problem-Solve

If your core purpose is radically out of alignment with your values and priority dimensions of wellness, then you might have to pause and problem-solve, and consider how to get the three areas in greater harmony. For example, I have to be actively engaged in paid employment or volunteer work to be able to implement Mission 2: To be of service to others and be a positive force in my community (Social & Spiritual). Although I am not growing my business, the Occupational Dimension still plays a supporting role. Besides, I enjoy working and I feel lost without the benefit of a daily schedule. Work gives meaning to my life, and gives me greater opportunity to serve other individuals and my larger community.

Step 4: Act & Implement

If you're satisfied with the plan you drafted, you have to act and implement a simple plan of action. Let's discuss and outline a concrete example to demonstrate how to do this step. How do I act and implement Mission 1. Let's review the action steps on the chart on the next page:

Step 5: Review & Redo

Since life is constantly changing, you might need to revisit your plan at least once a year. Moving from 60 to 70 years old is a major leap. Major physical, emotional, and financial changes occur as one ages from one decade to another. I review and modify my plan once a year during my birthday in January. I spend a couple of hours examining and reflecting on my life's purpose and modify this when a critical change occurs. For example, I cut down on my consulting work, from full time to part-time since my health was declining and I am approaching really "old, old age." I just settled for a single consulting contract to keep my mind engaged in intellectual work that gives me so much pleasure and contentment.

PURPOSE/MISSION	STRATEGIES: ACTION STEPS
To love and cherish my friends and family	To keep in touch (e.g., telephone, email, text, or any written form) with my sons and granddaughter at least once a week
	To share a meal with my sons once a month
	To actively listen to their concerns and share their joys and challenges
	To give them well thought-out advice, when asked
	To hold a family reunion (extended family) once a year.
	To travel with my sisters at least once a year
	To celebrate birthdays, anniversaries, & holidays together whenever possible (minimum of one special occasion per year)
	To keep in touch with my friends, at least bi-monthly
	To assist friends who are in need, share their joys and sorrows, and actively listen
	To show my love to my family and friends in various ways-from saying "I love you!" when saying "Goodbye!" over the telephone to "giving of my time and energy" when asked for help/ assistance

Model 2: A Simpler Planning Process

For those of you who prefer a simpler, no-frills step, which can be accomplished by doing a quick and cursory survey of the next chart (Figure 6 on the following page), the Seven Dimensions of Wellness and Well-Being, might appeal to you more. Imagine yourself having seven different rooms in your house. One or two might need major repairs, while others might be in reasonably good shape. Give the Seven Dimensions a rating of *Good, Fair, or Poor.* You might choose to do work on those you rated *Poor.* For example, you are now 80 years old and your priorities are shifting rapidly, as physical, emotional, and mental changes seem to be coming at a rapid-fire pace. You are not at all inclined to address and develop the Intellectual, Occupational, and Social

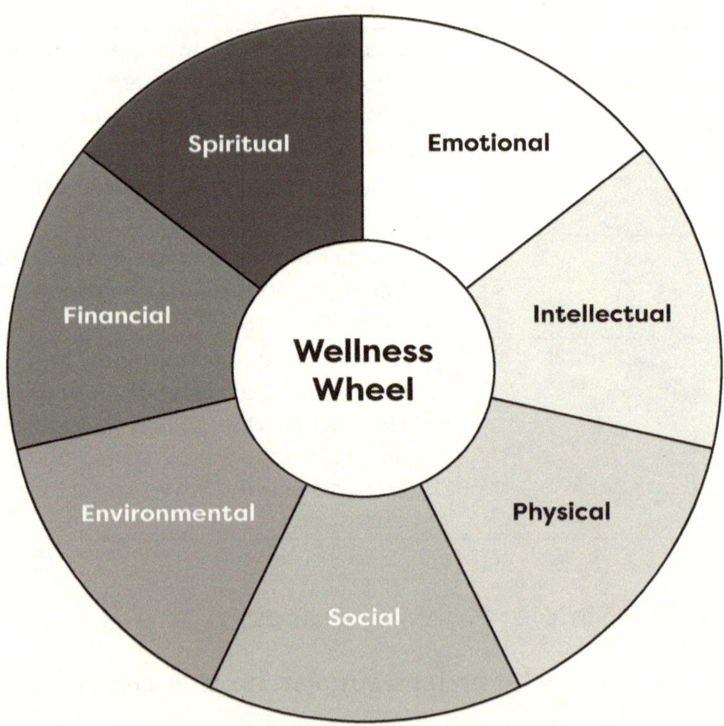

Figure 6: Seven Dimensions of Wellness–
Planning Wheel for Individuals 60 Years and Older

dimensions because you're mentally confused, suffering from a tired and foggy brain, and you are plagued with unrelenting physical exhaustion. If you're able to think clearly and plan, you or your family will most likely be focused on your need for quality care in a senior living facility, your financial ability to pay for whatever new housing arrangement you can afford, and other key factors affecting this unplanned move. You are now unable to take care of yourself, and cannot live independently. Do you go to an assisted living community, a nursing home, or a facility with memory care services? Planning at this juncture is futile; hence the need to draw up plans when you're in full possession of your faculties.

Community Living Choices for Seniors

Choosing a senior living community before you need to actually transition to one is a critical and time-consuming task that needs to be planned for. Depending on several factors, such as your health, financial ability, personal preferences, and other unique identifiers, you might choose living in an independent living community, assisted living, nursing home, or a facility that offers memory care services. Many seniors choose aging in place, which is staying and growing older at your home. Let's discuss this last option to demonstrate the factors you have to consider to successfully transition to this living arrangement.

Aging in Place: Growing Older at Home

When my friend Lita started to experience physical, emotional, and cognitive decline, she asked for help from her son, and mentioned that she feels less and less capable of taking care of herself. She remarked that cleaning the house, doing the laundry, shopping for food and other daily chores are getting to be too much for her. Despite all these challenges, Lita expressed her desire to stay in her home.

Robert, her oldest son, is the designated caregiver. He started doing his research by reviewing resources and information from the National Institute on Aging, the state's Division of Aging and Adults with Disabilities, local geriatric care managers, and referral sites for senior living. He collected all the information, did some online research, and then interviewed the local community experts in person. Armed with this knowledge, he mapped our areas that need to be addressed in order to support his mother's wish to age in place.

Planning for Present and Future Needs

Planning for his mother's current needs and requirements to be able to stay home alone is paramount in his mind. He is aware of some of her limitations due to osteoporosis, gastrointestinal problems, and anxiety issues. He hired a rehabilitation engineer to do some home modifications to prevent falls and fractures and enhance her mobility. For example, the two bathrooms were fitted with handrails to hold when taking a shower and a stable chair to sit on to eliminate slips and falls. The carpenter installed lower cabinets so his mother could reach all the cooking utensils, dishes, and silverware she needs to heat food and eat. A few other remodeling changes were made to make her house safer and easier to maneuver and help her continue to live alone independently.

Future needs and requirements have to be planned for as soon as present needs are addressed satisfactorily. Robert is aware that his mother is pre-diabetic, it appears to run in the family, so he made an appointment with her family physician to anticipate future needs. This arrangement appears to be a realistic and well-thought-out choice for his mother because she has lived in this neighborhood for more than fifty years. She has many friends in the area who provide her assistance with shopping, driving to doctors' visits, socializing, and going to restaurants.

Robert is also aware that his mother would need home care services sometime in the future to continue living at home. He searched out referral sites for senior living and found out that it would cost an average of $4,767 per month to hire a full-time home health aide or a homemaker. He would also need to check out nursing homes as an alternative when more intensive medical care is needed. All these are tasks that are primarily the responsibility of older adults, who need to initiate the planning, or at least take the lead in addressing how to plan for age-related decline. To keep their independence and to age gracefully, planning needs to be done years before. This way, they can be active participants in choosing the right path for them.

Resources and Supports Needed When Aging in Place

Personal Care and Meals: Right now, Lita is able to do the basic activities of daily living, such as doing her personal hygiene, dressing, and feeding herself. Since she has balance and dizziness problems, Robert contacted the local center to deliver meals for a voluntary contribution of $5.00 per meal. On Fridays, local restaurants donate nutritious and delicious food to eligible seniors, free of charge. Sometimes, Lita goes to the senior center to share a meal with a friend and to attend social events, such as concerts, special holiday gatherings, and lectures.

Household Chores: Lita has never been a good cook so Meals on Wheels was a brilliant choice. Robert hired an experienced cleaning woman, who has been cleaning for his neighbor's family for years. He also hired outside help to do the yard work. The cleaning woman is also open to the idea of driving Lita to the supermarket and the drugstore, when needed. Neighbors also volunteered to do quick runs for necessities for Lita.

Money Management: Lita is getting assistance from Robert's wife who is a financial consultant and an accountant. When it comes to managing money and paying bills, it's best to get a trusted relative or professional to do the tasks. Bills can be paid online and checks deposited directly to her account.

Socialization, strong connections, and loving relationships are crucial at this phase of the aging process. Change and transitions are life-changing, disconcerting, and confusing, especially for older adults who have lived in the same place for more than half their lives. Robert's diligence, love, and support for his mother has shifted us closer to a practical template of what needs to be done before we enter the door of old age. Do you have a plan for the next decade of your life?

CHAPTER 18

Positive Aging

Finding Purpose, Passion, and Joy in Old Age

How would you want to be referred to as an old person? I always try to develop a positive attitude and make healthy but realistic life choices. But when physical, mental, and emotional decline started to emerge, I wasn't ready for this stranger. It was like an uninvited guest just showing up, unannounced, in the middle of the night. It was my plan to age gracefully and defy expectations. But now I am saddled with these limitations that came so soon.

I am just eighty years old, and I already feel old and decrepit. True, the blasted cluster of symptoms started to show up years ago. My bones and muscles started to weaken as osteoporosis attempted to set in; but the CBD salve appears to have stopped its spread and reign, and daily exercise seems to have some positive effects. The gastrointestinal problems responded well with the use of proton pump inhibitors, like Nexium and Prilosec. But the dizziness, loss of balance, foggy brain, and fatigue—a cluster of symptoms, fortified with anxiety and fear, continue to plague me up to this day. My physician thinks these vague symptoms were ushered in by the pandemic and the predisposition to anxiety and fear—a genetic trait that I inherited from my mother. For almost three years now, I have been marinating in this toxic stew of dizzy spells, foggy brain, and exhaustion.

I have consulted with many physicians and specialists in Dover and Newark, Delaware, but they came up empty when it comes to a clear-cut diagnosis. Some of them peddled typical memes reflecting a popular diagnosis, when the doctor has no idea of what is truly going on with a patient. It is called medical gaslighting, which means that they are minimizing what I am feeling and attributing all the symptoms to my emotions because they are stumped for a diagnosis. If only they would listen to the patient, a good diagnostic tool, instead of typing on their computers, while ordering dozens of tests to help them with the diagnosis.

Do I mind being called "old," of course, I do if I have to endure these obstacles that are endemic with old age. Ask me again after I adjust my attitude and look at creative ways to cope with this hellacious lot.

Aging is inevitable—like death, taxes, and laundry, they are an integral part of life. As humans, we cannot escape this reality. Intellectually, I am aware of this brutal reality, but I was not prepared to get old, wither, and decay this fast. A sensation of doom and gloom is lapping at my feet, much like a rising tide about to drown me. Now, what should I do?

Changing Perspectives: Discovering the Positive Sides of Aging

I have been through worse scenarios before and I managed to survive and even thrive. I do not have to accept circumstances in my life that make me less than fulfilled and sometimes downright miserable and unhappy. I have grown weary of my chronic complaining and jaundiced point of view. I have gone totally crazy because I am unable to learn, teach, and write—my three favorite preoccupations. Finally, after close to a year and a half, I changed my mind's gravitational center and focused on the positive. I cannot stop aging but I certainly can choose how I react to age-related decline. Now, it is time to problem-solve and act.

I have consulted with doctors in my home state with minimal success, now it seems a good time to go cross-consult with experts and specialists in other states. I also dropped the denial and anger that spiced the transition to old age, and slid into the trial and experimentation stage. I found out that even if I am slightly dizzy, I can still walk, do the treadmill, and sometimes drive safely. I did my gaze stabilization exercises and the Epley maneuver that I learned from my physical therapist to address the dizziness and lack of balance. I pushed the boundaries with the foggy brain and realized that I can penetrate the "fog" through sheer focus, determination, and use of my overdeveloped muscle memory. This simple but elegant discovery allowed me to read and learn from my prized nonfiction books, start planning and researching my next book, and begin to write the first chapter in my book. I felt like a champion—I can do the tasks that I love the most. Engaging in these activities made me feel competent, happy, and alive! What a triumphant new beginning. I must continue taming this man-made wall, an artificial barrier built by this society, and a social imperative that I implicitly and mindlessly accepted.

Transitions: Our Culture is Focused on the Negative Side of Aging

Change is the only constant in life, and we all go through life transitions—from youth, to middle age, to old age, if we are lucky. There are negatives and positives, risks, and opportunities in all of life's passages, but our society appears to be entrenched in glorifying youth and casting a negative shadow on old age. We often hear about the physical, mental, and emotional challenges facing older people; the burden and responsibilities associated with caregiving elder parents; nursing home choices and expenses for aging parents, and other less benign stories about older people. Stories from aging adults reveal their feelings of anxiety and fear over their inability to cope, loss of autonomy, and value, especially after retirement. It appears that our society does not value the cumulative knowledge, wisdom, and experience of senior citizens. They struggle to find their place in the new world, where their roles and statuses are ambiguous, ill-defined, and of little value. Respect for elders is not a cherished value in this society. The phrase "old age" does not conjure any pleasant visual picture or kinesthetic vibrations. Most people in our society choose not to look "old." We dye our hair and refuse to go gray; wrinkles are stamped out with Botox, all kinds of moisturizing creams, gels, and formulas to stay looking youthful; and sometimes, we even resort to plastic surgery to preserve our youth. Looking old and old age are to be avoided at all cost. It is an unpleasant and depressing subject that we try to avoid.

Kory D. Miller *(Positive Aging,* March 8, 2019) states that societies "who revere their elders look to them for wisdom and guidance. These cultures don't see their elders as a burden or hindrance. They respect them." However, she notes that "Other cultures—those who value youth and physical beauty more than wisdom that can come with age—have a different perspective. Oftentimes, it's those in this group who choose to fight aging."

Positive Side of Aging: Opportunities for Growth

The past three years have been a time of challenges, trials, experimentation, and acceptance. There are times when I get impatient with myself and wonder when I will ever learn the not-so-secret realities of life. I have been through this journey before; I should have mastered the pattern and the evolving life phases that all humans go through. But life is so complex that humans sometimes fail to see the big picture when caught in the day-to-day routine of life. Once I embraced the negatives of old age and started to adapt to the limitations, the shiny side of the experience started to show its inimitable glow. What are opportunities presented by this chapter of life?

Positive aging is "The process of maintaining a positive attitude, feeling good about yourself, keeping fit and healthy, and engaging fully in life," according to the Positive Psychology Institute. Since I started to accept the reality of old age and took the first step, my resistance to the negative side of this life event is starting to lose its grip. Here are the positives that are slowly manifesting their presence and enigmatic face:

1. **Ability to learn new knowledge and experience:** This does not stop, even during old age. My quintessential number one

value is lifelong learning. I feel hopeful that my old *cabeza* is still working despite the foggy thinking, shorter time for higher level focus, and longer time for memory retrieval. Neuroplasticity, the ability of the brain to form and reorganize synaptic connections does not stop, even as we age. A synapse is a small gap at the end of a neuron that allows a neuron to transmit information from one neuron to the next Kendra Cherry, (*What is a Synapse,* September 10, 2022).

Kory D. Miller (*Positive Aging,* March 8, 2019) explains that "The plasticity in the older brain is in a different area than in younger brains. In older brains, the change is in the

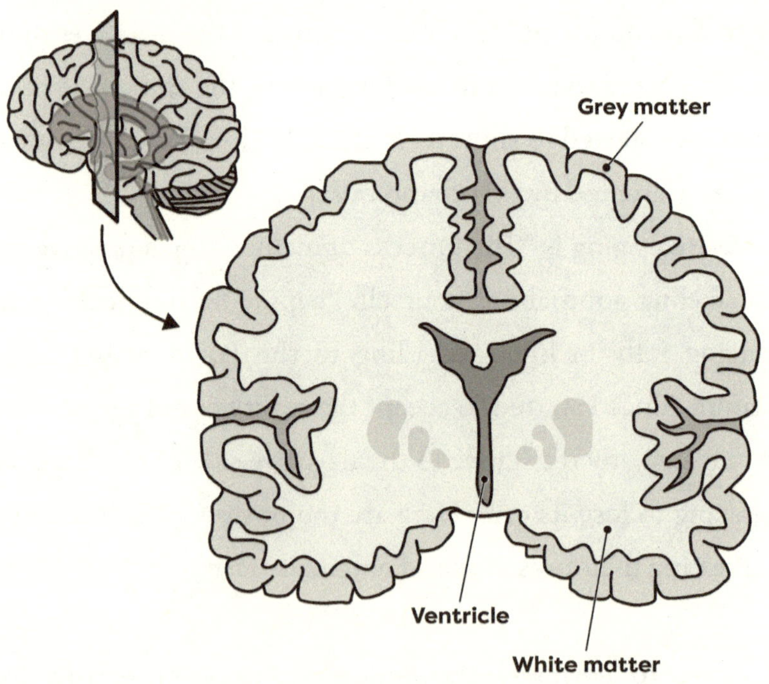

Figure 7: White Matter of the Brain

white matter. White matter houses the brain's axons covered in myelin. Myelin makes the transfer of signals faster." Myelin sheath is a whitish-fatty substance that covers axons and is the reason for the white appearance of the white matter.

Olivia Guy Evans *(White Matter in the Brain,* October 11, 2021) explains that "The central nervous system (CNS) is made up of tissue known as white matter and grey matter. White matter makes up around half of the brain and is comprised of bundles of millions of axons (or nerve fibers). White matter is located in the deep parts of the brain while grey matter makes up the outer surface of the brain." The white and grey matter are depicted in Figure 7.

2. Wisdom, Purpose, and Creativity: Cumulative wisdom gained through years of living, surviving, and thriving is a protective factor that makes it easier to navigate whatever complexities and barriers life throws at you. The shorter life span remaining forces you to focus on what's critical and important, like relationships and a compelling purpose in life. When you wake up in the morning, there's something of value to do to make time go smoother and faster. Young folks do not have a monopoly on creativity and innovation. Now that I am old and my cognitive skills, attention span, and memory retrieval are slower and possibly less powerful, I am starting to reinvent myself. Maybe, I can write a

> book of stories, instead of a single topic book project; or do individual leadership coaching instead of working for an entire organization to improve performance. During this old-age period, I was able to develop and test a new leadership model for women, minorities, and people with disabilities. Of course, I had tons of help from colleagues, friends, and other women who felt as invested in the process as I am. Creativity is still alive and sparkling, despite decline in some areas. Crystallized intelligence made the reinvention so much easier and spectacularly fulfilling. It almost felt robotic, making the instantaneous connections—from awareness to analysis and synthesis—with magical precision and speed. Who says creativity is the purview of the young?

Crystallized intelligence and *cognitive reserve* are two key attributes that old people possess that allow them to improve cognitive performance. *Crystallized intelligence* is the ability to combine learned knowledge with experience to handle new problems and tasks, especially those that have similar and comparable processes. For example, I can apply my knowledge of organizational strategic planning to plan my life for the next decade. This step can benefit me as I explore the unknown future and map out a path that is realistic and meaningful. *Cognitive reserve* refers to "your brain's ability to improvise and find alternate ways of getting a job done. Just like a powerful car that enables you to engage another gear and suddenly accelerate to avoid an obstacle, your brain can change the way it operates and thus make added resources available to cope with challenges. Cognitive reserve is developed by a lifetime of education and curiosity to help your brain better cope with any failures or declines it faces. (*What is Cognitive Reserve?* Harvard Medical School, 2021).

3. **Level of Happiness:** Happiness is a choice. I cannot stop the process of aging and many unfortunate incidents that might happen to me, but I certainly can choose how to react to them, problem-solve, and stay fairly happy and satisfied. Studies have shown that older adults are happier than younger adults *(Journal of Clinical Psychiatry),* despite declining physical, mental, and emotional health. A study done by Stanford University on the psychology of aging indicates that the majority of seniors are happier because the wisdom of experience has taught them to focus on what's important to them, such as meaningful, resilient, and strong connections and relationships. Having strong and loving relationships with family and friends is the number one reason that made people who live alone happy during the different stages of life from youth to old age (del Tufo, *SoloPower,* 2014). Enriching relationships offer a protective armor when life throws you a curveball and minimizes the loneliness experienced during this chapter in your life.

Transition Phases of Old Age

I think it might be worthwhile to share a tentative concept of the different phases that individuals go through as they transition to this chapter in their lives. I tested this model with a handful of individuals whom I consider as fairly happy and adjusted oldies. It makes me feel more comfortable, less anxious, and more open to life's changes when I am able to anticipate what lies ahead. It's also comforting to know that other individuals are experiencing the same or similar upheavals and life changes that I am going through.

Below are my reflections on the different phases that I went through these past couple of years, which in my 60s and early 70s were gradual and incremental, and accelerated at a rapid pace during my late 70s.

Phase 1: Confusion and Loss of Identity

After I retired from my consulting job, I started to experience some degree of confusion, loss of identity, and isolation. Of course, the pandemic exacerbated this feeling of isolation and aloneness. It was, however, deeper than the emotional trauma precipitated by the pandemic. I felt completely lost, with no schedules and deadlines, and no compelling reasons to wake up in the morning. The absence of intellectual nourishment was devastating. I live in my brain; I am totally disconnected from the world around me when my brain is disengaged. Not engaging in formal work left me with a blank slate—I lost not only the *social role* that I played more than half my life, but also the corresponding *social status* that work engenders. I felt angry at myself for feeling this insecure and for allowing myself to be simply defined by my career. Certainly, the identity contours and essence of my life are far richer, deeper, and fuller than a job! I was a wife, a mother, a friend, a volunteer, an author, a community activist, and more.

Phase 2: Experimentation and Discovery

Who am I, I often asked myself during those challenging times. You were a child of war, a young widow, an immigrant, and a woman of color. Your nerves of steel have been forged in adversity and suffering. Pick yourself up and rise up to the age of elderhood. Every morning, I would wake up looking for nourishment for my empty brain, and a structure to house my emerging idea of a plan. Looking out my bay window, I felt like the red fox in my backyard, sniffing for prey, and ready to pounce at anything for its next meal. I had a short list of ideas that I started to fly around, but I was guided by this malignant form of common sense, which appears to be devoid of reality. I planned on escaping the monotony of it all by taking a trip to my favorite spot in Italy. Brilliant idea! You could barely walk a straight line, with the balance issue and the dizziness getting a bit worse. Scrap that idea. Now, I tried to be realistic and logical, and eased into the problem-solving mode.

I started to calm down and look at simple realities, like I have a blank page as my canvas; how lucky for me! I can be as creative as I would like to be. Go back and learn from the past. What is it that I value the most about what I did before? I know I absolutely enjoy learning, teaching, coaching, doing research, and of course, writing. I reminded myself that I have robust crystallized intelligence and versatile cognitive reserve that more than compensate for the decline that comes with age. I also have a lifetime of key knowledge and learning from advanced education, continuing research, application, and other hands-on-experience that form a powerful cluster of crystallized intelligence that I can apply to new tasks and other future endeavors. I have enough resources to plot my future and determine my own meaningful path.

Phase 3: Acceptance, Comfort, and Some Degree of Control

After the initial confusion and shock that overwhelmed me, I was able to gather my wits and cut down on the anxiety loops. I cleared my mind, and started to heal and survive. As Dr. Agronin reminds us, "we can tap into our past strengths and inspiration" and begin to see "possibilities instead of problems." His major message, which he learned from Dr. Gene D. Cohen, founding father of geriatric psychiatry, is the possibility of accomplishing new and rich experiences "not in spite of aging, but because of aging." Aging is itself the spark that motivates older people to go into untrodden land, experiment new ways of doing things, and come up with an accidental discovery that brings new life, novelty, and meaning to their barren lives.

After doing an inventory of my past strengths and weakness, I started to tap into the skills and competencies that made me happy, fulfilled, and reasonably successful. So instead of writing a 200-page book, I penned a 500-word commentary for the local newspaper. Then, I resumed writing poetry, which appealed to my passions, my heart, and my right brain that needed attention and exercise. I also learned how to pace myself and not work twenty-four hours a day, but take a short break by listening to music, dancing a few rounds of rock 'n roll, or having a relaxing conversation with a friend. I designated Fridays as my "no-worries day" and Sunday as a "day of rest." Despite the cluster of debilitating symptoms that continue to plague me, I am still able to write a book, do a video of my book on *Women Powered!* and complete a book of poetry. The pleasant and relaxing smell of comfort and contentment are beginning to envelop my sweet space. Gone are the spirals of obsessive thoughts about what this or that symptom could mean, instead I consult with a specialist if it feels serious, face it, and be done with it. As Ryan Holiday *(What About Time? Daily Stoics,* July 18, 2022) reminds us "Each of us is on this earth for an uncertain and finite period." Enjoy the sublime pleasure of the moment; feel the visceral joy of being alive!

Parting Words

What the caterpillar calls the end,
the rest of the world calls a butterfly. —Lao Tsu

I stand in support of Dr. Agronin's thesis on positive aging and I, too, reject the idea that old age is the harbinger of primarily negative life experiences, such as cognitive and physical decline. Despite the losses and limitations of old age, it can usher in a new universe of existence where what is important in life is made crystal clear; where stillness and reflections allow us to enjoy the moment and hear our hearts' songs; where material things become irrelevant; where self-promotion is not the reason for being, but rather service to others and love of family. Although my hearing and eyesight are impaired, I can see universal truths more clearly and hear the voice inside me more acutely. Old age appears to bring what's truly important in life into sharper focus. Happiness is a state of mind and it is a choice available to everyone.

In his nationally acclaimed book *The End of Old Age: Living a Longer, More Purposeful Life* (2018), Dr. Marc Agronin presents a more hopeful view of the aging process, casting it as a developmental force that brings unique strengths, including wisdom, purpose, and creativity. This change in paradigm to a more affirming vision of old age can be self-fulfilling, he observes. He concludes that "This mind-body connection is really profound. To a large extent, we age to our expectations."

CHAPTER 19

The Two Faces of Capitalism

ALL SYSTEMS, CONCEPTS, and ideas are value-neutral—they succeed or fail, they become good or bad, depending on actual implementation or deployment experience, achievement of strategic goals and objectives, and targeted outcomes. Capitalism is an economic system that has been adopted by the United States and most European countries. It is an economic approach that is based on the private ownership of the means of production, which are run for profits. The manufacture of goods and commodities is done by workers, who work for a salary or wages. Key characteristics of capitalism include capital accumulation, competitive markets, price system, private property, property rights, voluntary exchange, and wage labor (*Capitalism:* Wikipedia, 2022).

In the late 20th century, traditional capitalism appears to have morphed into an undesirable form of economic system, where profit is the central focus and singular goal for all involved. Edward Paul Lazear (*Socialism, Capitalism, and Income,* May 26, 2020) noted that "A country that has a small proportion of very wealthy people coupled with a large group of very poor people is not what most would judge as a desirable country." In the United States, there is a massive gap between the rich and the poor. According to an article written by Senator Bernie Sanders for *Guardian* magazine (*The Gap Between the Rich and the Poor Is Obscene,* March 29, 2021), "In 1978, the top 0.1 percent owned about 7 percent of the nation's wealth. In 2019, the latest year of data available, they own nearly 20 percent . . . Unbelievably, the two richest people in America, Jeff Bezos and Elon Musk, now own more wealth than the bottom 40 percent of Americans combined."

A new form of capitalism, benevolent capitalism, is showing its enigmatic face, which appears to cause some cosmic reshuffling in the predatory capitalism system that has dominated the economic landscape for decades. For any institution to survive and flourish, it has to accommodate the changing needs of its customers and stakeholders. Continuous improvement is demanded by those most affected by it, some powerful practitioners and business leaders, governmental entities, and some political leaders.

Traditional (Free-Market, Free Enterprise, or Laissez-Faire) Capitalism and Greed

It might be noble and even patriotic to think that *free enterprise capitalism* is good for the economic prosperity of the country because it results in high productivity, and consequently higher wages for workers. As can be gleaned by looking at data in the United States, there remains a great disparity between the rich and the poor. Free enterprise has also been inextricably linked to political freedom in a democracy, an apparent effort to disguise the unilateral goal of making as much money as humanly possible for a single entity. The economic driver—gaining profits unabated by governmental intervention, became part of the collective American psyche, and was justified in support of personal freedom, economic growth, and a democratic society. The outcomes do not appear to validate this synaptic connection between capitalism and democracy. On the contrary, it has resulted in the widening gap between the rich and the poor due to rising income inequality, as can be gleaned in the data and Figure 8 on page 173 (*Federal Reserve Board Survey of Consumer Finances,* 2019). This survey is the gold standard for information on wealth in America and is conducted every three years. The 2019 report was published in 2020.

"In 2019, total wealth had grown to $96.1 trillion. The 2019 population was approximately 129 million families.

- To be in the top 10 percent, a family needed $1.22 million or more (slightly less than in 2016). Together, these roughly 12.9 million wealthy families owned 76 percent of total household wealth in 2019.

- To be in the middle 40 percent, a family needed at least $122,000 in wealth. Together, these approximately 51.5 million families owned 22 percent of U.S. wealth in 2019.

- To be in the bottom 50 percent meant a family had less than $122,000 in wealth. That represented about 64.3 million, or half of families in 2019, owning just 1 percent of the nation's wealth. Further, of this group, some 13.4 million families (about 1 in 10) had negative net worth—they didn't even have a slice of the pie."

The report concludes that overall wealth (i.e., what a family owns minus debts) inequality remains high among American families.

Author Raymond Smith (*The Role of Greed in the Ongoing Global Financial Crisis,* November 2010) points out that greed and insensitivity to the needs of others are "corrosive values" that are enriching a few at the expense of many, and have resulted in the global financial crisis in 2007–2009. A book by Dr. Paul

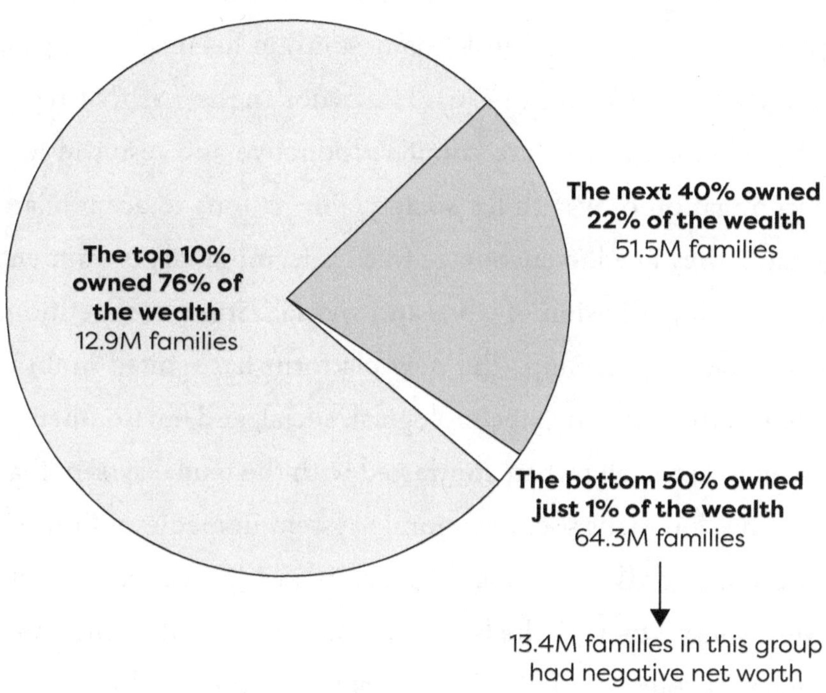

Figure 8: Wealth Distribution Among American Families

Mazzola, *Countdown to the Global Financial Crisis* (2022, Cambridge Scholars), echoes a similar conclusion. Mazzola states that "Exploitation of customers, the misalignment of governance frameworks and practices, and the profit driven performance incentives which drive self-interest combine to maintain a culture underpinned by power and greed." He also reminds us that unless the dysfunctional behaviors of business leaders are modified, the world is bound to experience similar economic debacles in the near future and beyond.

The concept of capitalism was introduced by Scottish moral philosopher and economist Adam Smith in his magnum opus, *The Wealth of Nations* (1776). His major thesis was that regulations on commerce are counterproductive and result in less accumulation of wealth for society. For nations to accumulate wealth, they need to encourage free trade, minimal government intervention, division of labor and specialization, competition, and private ownership. The new platform has ignited innovations in the industrial, technological, social, and environmental spheres, especially when contrasted with the feudal system that was the dominant socio-economic system in medieval Europe. The feudal lords held lands for the crown while peasants or serfs were obliged to work the land in exchange for food, shelter, and military protection. In a BBC report by Matthew Wilburn King (*Why the Next Stage of Capitalism is Coming,* May 26, 2021), he reminded us that capitalism, which evolved significantly during the ensuing centuries, resulted in an open society, rule of law, freedom of expression, and free market policies. Ordinary citizens were granted private property rights, personal choice, greater individual freedom, and civil liberties.

In the 1980s, the newer version of capitalism pushed for free trade, lower taxes on income and capital, and minimal regulation from the government, which increased economic growth worldwide. Milton Friedman, an American economist and author of *Capitalism and Freedom* (1962), profoundly influenced this new direction of capitalism. He believed that free market capitalism with minimal government intervention is the only way to increase value for all stakeholders and to optimize freedom for all. He served as an advisor to President Ronald Reagan and British Prime Minister Margaret Thatcher.

Benevolent Capitalism

If it isn't broken, break it and make it better. Business paradigms, models, or systems have a life cycle, and during times of rapid and unrelenting change, the old paradigm quickly becomes obsolete and irrelevant. This is true of conventional capitalism currently practiced by business leaders and criticized by customers and stakeholders. Its old mission of focusing on profits at all costs, which borders on greed, has lost its Midas luster, and an emerging new model is evolving from the Friedman style of capitalism that enriches a few at the expense of many.

Daniel Flynn of *Venture* magazine (Quarter 2, 2021 Issue) frames the current problem now confronting the business world in the paragraph that follows:

"At the moment, too many business endeavors tend to be about enriching the few at the expense of the many. Enriching the few is not so much the problem, it is more the at the expense of the many. . . However, if leaders choose to align the capitalism maxim with the maxim of a sustainable future for people and planet, there are still abundant possibilities and revenues to be actualised—revenues made in ways that generate a sustainable future rather than damage the planet and endanger our future. This is benevolent capitalism." The article claims that benevolent capitalism is the new platform that can create a better world and optimize value for all business leaders and stakeholders.

The discussion below is an exploration of the initial statements of business leaders, who are pioneering the benevolent capitalism platform. It is my interpretation of their published documents, where authors are not even identified. I suspect, this movement is at the beginning stages of a socio-economic system, where a collective effort is emerging to define a new paradigm, with the potential of introducing systemic changes to the present system. The pioneers might need to do several coordinated and expert-led strategic planning sessions, where diverse stakeholders engage in defining their mission, vision, broad goals, measurable objectives, and key performance outcomes. I get the feeling that the pioneers are still contemplating as to why they exist, where they are taking us with this innovation, and what objectives and goals they are pursuing.

The Four Priorities of Benevolent Capitalism

1. **Generate a sustainable future:** The benevolent capitalism's mission goes beyond simply maximizing profits for investors and company leaders by focusing on the strategic goal

of generating a sustainable future for all through social responsibility and governance. This means that financial performance is no longer the single measure for success, but also how the business contributes to the betterment of society and the environment where it operates. If the pioneers follow through on this unifying goal, they could develop performance measures for success, which might include the following outcome perspectives: financial, environmental, human or social, political, and civil liberties. The goal is not simply survival of societies and the environment, but that people and the environment get better, grow, and thrive within an inclusive society and have a sustainable future.

2. Do no damage to society and the environment: This second priority is inextricably tied to and aligned with the first. The approach dictates not only positive outcomes and sustainability, but also the deliberate avoidance of negative and harmful consequences (intended or unintended) to society and the planet.

3. Maximize possibilities for all, not just profits for some: This priority is a clear divergence from the Friedman dogma of increasing profits as capitalism's singular goal for only the business owners and its investors, and expands the cone of benefits to workers, stakeholders, and to different levels of society. It is a priority that is based on the interconnectedness

of a system—what happens to a component of the system impacts the whole. The players within a unified system are not distinct nor separate; they are intimately connected.

4. **Empowerment of all through benevolent leadership:** The system is powered by a leader who models the ideals of benevolent leadership through action and supports the collective growth survival, prosperity, and betterment of all people, societies, and the natural environment. His/her actions are guided by his/her concern for others and for the common good.

These four priorities are modeled by business leaders like Bill Gates of Microsoft Corporation, Ben and Jerry's, Peloton, and others, where they use a significant portion of their profits to benefit their employees, communities, societies, and the world. Mark Cuban, celebrity entrepreneur, Dallas Maverick owner, and star of ABC's *Shark Tank,* confirms that capitalism is not simply about making as much money as one can. He also firmly believes that "Capitalism is about finding solutions to problems and seeing what you can do to solve them." In a recent article written by Charlotte Alter (*Time* magazine, *Celebrity Entrepreneur Mark Cuban is taking on Big Pharma,* December 5–12, 2022), Cuban recalls how he collaborated with Dr. Alex Oshmyansky, a radiologist to launch a for-profit pharmaceutical company—*Cost Plus Drugs,* to compete with greedy pharmaceutical companies, who are charging usurious prices to customers. He explains that "*Cost Plus Drugs* is a kind of middle-path between progressive reform and philanthropic giving, one that aims to disrupt predatory markets as a way of regulating them." In essence, Cuban is using competition and disruption to modify the negative face of capitalism. He is also successfully managing risks inherent in disruption by making certain that there is a viable option to replace the existing model—one that can compete and deliver a quality replacement to the present business model. It appears that this brand of capitalism is here to stay, as business leaders collaborate with experts in other fields to generate vibrant and innovative ideas and models to modulate the excesses of the present system.

Parting Words

Despite massive and continuing criticisms of capitalism, it appears to remain a strong and viable economic system as it continues to spread across the globe. It is a shiny object that offers individual and collective freedom and wealth, and the promise of economic prosperity for all. Our country is at an inflection point where we need to rethink and reshape the future configuration of capitalism as its promise of wealth, prosperity, safety, and power is enjoyed by a vital few, while the rest languish in poverty, hopelessness, and defeat. Socialism does not seem to be an attractive choice for most Americans. It has a tarnished reputation and its values and beliefs are not aligned with the American national character and values of freedom, individualism, competition, materialism, and altruism. Making profits, creating wealth, while helping those who have less, and creating a sustainable future for people and the environment can all co-exist. It requires the rethinking of capitalism, with the *mission* of uplifting the economic, social, political, and environmental perspectives for all and a *compelling vision* of co-creating a sustainable future for everyone. All these and more align so perfectly with benevolent capitalism.

The critical task of rethinking capitalism as it continues to evolve is of utmost importance—it crackles with urgency that needs to be addressed; some people feel left out and excluded. The oppression has reached a boiling point that exploded in the Halls of Congress. Armed with a unifying mission and a compelling vision, we might just turn this enterprise around, and ignite innovative ideas full of positive possibilities. The January 6 insurrection is a warning sign of the palpable discontent felt by a critical mass of people who felt left out, whose needs, wants, and dreams are unmet and dismissed as rebellious and inconsequential. Let's pause and reflect: Is this a symptom of a greater societal malaise, a cancer that will grow if left untreated?

Matthew Wilburn King of BBC warns us that "Ultimately, it is worth remembering that citizens in a capitalist, liberal democracy are *not powerless.* Collectively, they can support companies aligned with their beliefs and continuously demand new laws and policies which transform the competitive landscape of corporations so that they might improve their practices." And these are the benign responses, which could escalate to more violent and destructive acts of rebellion and insurrection. The feelings of injustice, anger, and hopelessness are corrosive emotions that could ignite into a full-blown revolution of the proletariat.

Business leaders might need to reflect more deeply and deliberately on the choices they are making, as they forge a path for a new and hopeful possibility for a more inclusive world. They need to confront and respond to critical questions of purpose, meaning, and legacy, such as: How can I be a catalyst for change and modify the way I do business so that it benefits all people, and avoids unintended harmful consequences for all creatures and the environment? What would this system look like? What goals, objectives, activities, and projected outcomes do I need to factor in to move the needle to realize a better future for all? These and other existential questions and actions are the challenges that benevolent leaders must face now to paint a compelling vision for their company and the world.

Bill Gates of Microsoft fame, invited the titans of industry to join him in harnessing the power of capitalism for the betterment of all citizens, with these inspiring words, "We have to find a way to make the aspects of capitalism that serve wealthier people serve poorer people as well."

References

Agronin, Dr. Marc E. (2018). *The End of Old Age: Living a Longer, More Purposeful Life*. Boston, Massachusetts: Da Capo Lifelong Books.

Alter, Charlotte. "*Celebrity Entrepreneur Mark Cuban is Taking on Big Pharma,*" *Time* magazine (December 5–12, 2022), pp. 26-27.

Associated Press. *Nearly 1 Million Covid Deaths: A Look at the Numbers.* Retrieved on May 14, 2022 from https://www.usnews.com/news/health-news/articles/2022-05-06/nearly-1-million-covid-19-deaths-a-look-at-the-us-numbers.

Assessing the Effects of COVID-19 on the Loneliness and Isolation of Older Adults. Retrieved on May 14, 2022 from https://covidresearch.ucsf.edu/projects/assessing-effect-covid-19-loneliness-and-social-isolation-older-adults.

Ausubel, Jacob. (March 10, 2020). *Older People are More Likely to Live Alone in the U.S. Than Elsewhere in the World.* Pew Research Center. Retrieved on July 26, 2022 from https://www.pewresearch.org/fact-tank/2020/03/10/older-people-are-more-likely-to-live-alone-in-the-u-s-than-elsewhere-in-the-world.

Bellah, Robert. (1991). *The Good Society*. Broadway, New York, New York: Knopf Doubleday Publishing Group.

Blanchard, Beverly. (April 3, 2013). *Law of Duality.* Retrieved on December 27, 2023 from https://beverlyblanchard.blogspot.com/2013/04/the-law-of-duality.html.

Britannica. *Yin Yang: Definition, Meaning, and Facts.* Retrieved on May 25, 2022 from www.britannica.com/topic/yinyang.

Brody E. Jane. (March 19, 2018). *Finding Meaning and Happiness in Old Age, New York Times.* Retrieved on September 15, 2022 from https://www.nytimes.com/2018/03/19/well/finding-meaning-and-happiness-in-old-age.html.

Byrne, John, H., ed. (2008). *Learning and Memory: A Comprehensive Reference.* Cambridge, Massachusetts: Academic Press, An Imprint of Elsevier, Inc.

Capitalism. Wikipedia. Retrieved on December 19, 2022 from https://en.wikipedia.org/wiki/capitalism.

Carroll, S. (October 18, 2013). *Is Time Real? Retrieved* on August 18, 2022 from https://www.preposterousuniverse.com/blog/2013/10/18/is-time-real.

Cherry, Kendra. (February 23, 2022). *What is a Collectivist Culture? Individualism Versus Collectivism.* Retrieved on August 2, 2022 from https://www.verywellmind.com/what-are-collectivistic-cultures-2794962.

Cherry, Kendra. (September 10, 2022). *What is a Synapse? Where Nerve Impulses are Passed from Neuron to Neuron.* Retrieved on September 1, 2022 from https://www.verywellhealth.com/synapse-anatomy-2795867.

Cohen, Gene D. (2001). *Creative Aging: Awakening Human Potential in the Second Half of Life.* New York, New York: William Morrow Paperbacks.

Curry, Hamish. (August 10, 2020). *The Purposes of Education.* Retrieved on July 3, 2022 from http://hamishcurry.com/2020/08/10/the-four-purposes-of-education.

del Tufo, Theresa. (2017). *Behind the Golden Door: The Resilience of Today's Immigrants.* Melbourne, Florida: Motivational Press.

del Tufo, Theresa. (2014). *SoloPower: How to Harness the Secret Energy of Living Alone.* Melbourne, Florida: Motivational Press.

del Tufo, Theresa. (2015). *The Fullness of Nothing: Discover the Hidden Joy that Surrounds You.* Melbourne, Florida: Motivational Press.

del Tufo, Theresa & George Banez. (2021). *Women Powered! A New Paradigm of Influence and Equity.* Jefferson, North Carolina: Toplight, an imprint of MacFarland & Company Publishers.

Domhoff, G. William. (2005). *Who Rules America? Power, Politics and Social Change.* New York, New York: McGraw-Hill.

Durkheim, Emile. (1893). *The Division of Labor in Society.* The Free Press, New York.

Felsenthal, Edward. (November 23, 2020). *Our Dueling American Realities Remain. Time* magazine. Retrieved on November 30, 2020 from time.com/author/edward-felsenthal.

Friedman, Milton. (1962). *Capitalism and Freedom.* Chicago, Illinois: University of Chicago Press.

Guy-Evans, O. (May 9, 2021). *Amygdala Function and Location.* Simply Psychology. www.simplypsychology.org/amygdala.html.

Guy-Evans, Olivia. (October 11, 2021). *White Matter in the Brain.* Retrieved on September 1, 2022 from https://www.simplypsychology.org/what-is-white-matter-in-the-brain.html.

Gurrentz and Yeris Mayol-Garcia. (April 22, 2021). *Marriage, Divorce, Widowhood Remain Prevalent Among Older Populations.* Retrieved on July 23, 2022 from https://www.census.gov/content/dam/Census/library/stories/2021/04/love-and-loss-among-older-adults-figure-1.jpg.

Hamermesh, Daniel, S., Michal Myck, and Monika Oczkowska. (May 19, 2021). *The Challenging Plight of Widows.* Retrieved on July 23, 2022 from https://wol.iza.org/opinions/the-challenging-plight-of-widows.

Harvard Medical School. (December 16, 2021). *What is Cognitive Reserve?* Retrieved on September 19, 2022 from https://www.health.harvard.edu/mind-and-mood/what-is-cognitive-reserve.

Haupt, Angela. (November 20, 2023). *Five Ways to Cultivate Hope When You Don't Have Any. Time* magazine.

Hill, Robert, D. (2008). *Seven Strategies for Positive Aging.* New York, New York: Norton Professionals.

Hernandez Kent, Ana & Lowell R. Ricketts. December 2, 2022. *Has Wealth Inequality in America Changed Over Time? Here are Key Statistics.* Retrieved on December 19, 2022 from https://www.stlouisfed.org/open-vault/2020/december/has-wealth-inequality-changed-over-time-key-statistics.

Holiday, Ryan. *Remember This Always, Daily Stoics.* Retrieved on May 25, 2022 from https://dailystoic.com/remember-you-dont-control-what-happens-you-control-how-you-respond.

Holiday, Ryan. (2019). *Stillness is the Key.* New York, New York: Penguin Random House.

Human Rights Watch. (January 24, 2017). Zimbabwe*: Widows Deprived of Property Rights.* Retrieved on July 20, 2022 from https://www.hrw.org/news/2017/01/24/zimbabwe-widows-deprived-property-rights).

Importance of Education in the Philippines. Retrieved on July 4, 2022 from https://www.imbalife.com/importance-of-education-in-the-philippines.

Jones, Kim. (August 15, 2012). *What is the Purpose of Education?* Retrieved on July 4, 2022 from https://www.forbes.com/sites/sap/2012/08/15/what-is-the-purpose-of-education/?sh=33834ab67795.

Kaplan, Daniel, B. and Berkman, Barbara J. (March 2021*). Older Adults Living Alone.* Merck Manual: Professional Version. Retrieved on July 22, 2022 from https://www.merckmanuals.com/professional/geriatrics/social-issues-in-older-adults/older-adults-living-alone.

King, Martin Luther. *A Tough Mind and a Tender Heart.* Retrieved on May 25, 2022 from https://kinginstitute.stanford.edu/king-papers/documents/tough-mind-and-tender-heart.

Kintsugi.(2015). Wikipedia, The Free Encyclopedia. Retrieved on May 6, 2022 from https://en.wikipedia.org/w/index.php?title=Kintsugi&oldid=683186968.

Kubler-Ross. (1969). *On Death and Dying.* Simon & Schuster.

Leahy, Robert L. (2005). *The Worry Cure: Seven Steps to Stop Worry from Worrying You.* New York, New York: Three Rivers Press.

Leland, John, Dr. (2018). *Happiness Is a Choice You Make: Lessons from a Year Among the Oldest Old.* New York, New York: Sarah Crichton Books.

Macionis, John, J. (2013*). Sociology* (15th Edition). Bloomington, Minnesota: Pearson Publisher.

Miller, Kory, D. (March 8, 2019). *Positive Aging: 10+ Principles to Shift Beliefs*

Around Age. Retrieved on September 10, 2022 from https://positivepsychology.com/positive-aging.

Mental Health America. *Depression in Older Adults: More Facts.* Retrieved on July 23, 2022 from www.mhanational.org/depression-older-adults.

Merton, R.K. (1938). Social Structure and Anomie. *American Sociological Review* 3, 672–682.

Muller, Wayne. (2013). *Legacy of the Heart.* New York, New York: Simon & Schuster, Inc.

Nickerson, C. (September 28, 2021). *Anomie Theory.* Simply Psychology. www.simplypsychology.org/anomie.html.

Norcross JC, Koocher GP, Garofalo A. (October 2006). "Discredited psychological treatments and tests: A Delphi poll". Professional Psychology: Research and Practice. 37 (5): 515–522. doi:10.1037/0735-7028.37.5.515. S2CID 35414392.

Punctuated Equilibrium. Retrieved from https://biologydictionary.net/punctuated-equilibrium.

Richardson, Thomas, M., et al. (April 2012). *Depression and its Correlates Among Older Adults Accessing Aging Services.* American Journal of Geriatric Psychiatry. Retrieved on July 26, 2022 from https://www.ncbi.nlm.nih.gov/pmc/articles/PMC3126880.

Psychology Today. (May 2, 2023). *The Power of Hope: The Secret Is Focusing on What You Can Control.* Retrieved on November 12, 2023 from https://www.psychologytoday.com/us/articles/202305/the-power-of-hope.

Salzman, C. Daniel (February 27, 2019). *Amygdala.* Encyclopedia Britannica. https://www.britannica.com/science/amygdala.

Sanders, Bernie. (March 29, 2021). *The Gap between the Rich and the Poor is Obscene.* Retrieved on December 19, 2022 from https://www.theguardian.com/commentisfree/2021/mar/29/rich-poor-gap-wealth-inequality-bernie-sanders.

Substance Abuse and Mental Health Services Administration, SAMHSA. (2022). *Eight Dimensions of Wellness.* Retrieved on September 30, 2022 from https://store.samhsa.gov/sites/default/files/d7/priv/sma16-4953.pdf.

Smith, Adam. (1776). *The Wealth of Nations.* Lincolnshire, Illinois: Legare Street Press.

Smith, William. *The Psychology of Grief: The Four Stages Explained.* Retrieved from https://positivepsychology.com/grief-stages/on November 12, 2023.

Spector, Nicole. (November 26, 2018). *Why our sense of time speeds up as we age and how to slow it down.* Retrieved on August 18, 2022 from https://www.nbcnews.com/better/health/why-our-sense-time-speeds-we-age-how-slow-it-ncna936351.

Spock, Benjamin. (1968). *Baby and Child Care* (Revised Edition). Gloucestershire, UK: Hawthorn Press.

Umebinyuo, Ijeoma. (2016). *Questions for Ada.* Middletown, Delaware.

Sutter, Paul. *What is Time?* (April 5, 2022). Retrieved on August 18, 2022, from https://www.livescience.com/what-is-time.

USA Facts on Crime and Justice. *Is the Criminal Justice System Working? Is the Country Getting Safer?* Retrieved on August 3, 2022 from https://usafacts.org/state-of-the-union/crime.

Violent Crimes in America. (September 30, 2021). Statista Research Department. Retrieved on August 3, 2022 from www.statista.com/topics/1750/violent-crime-in-the-us.

Wilburn King, Matthew. (May 26, 2021). *Why the Next Stage of Capitalism is Coming.* Retrieved on December 18, 2022 from https://www.bbc.com/future/article/20210525-why-the-next-stage-of-capitalism-is-coming.

Acknowledgments

I WROTE MOST OF THE CHAPTERS in this book during the COVID-19 pandemic, when the workplace was in virtual lockdown and I had more discretionary time. My son Joe suggested that I start writing a book or pursuing my consulting contracts. He knows that I function best when I am engaged and busy using my brain. My second son Mike, like Joe, always supported my passions and believed in my ability to pursue whatever goals I set for myself. My boys are my major motivators and guides, whenever I engage in any adventure. There is this magical and primal cohesion that bind us together as a family and as a creative team. I am most thankful to Joe for the magnificent book cover of the Buddha in Lahaina, Maui, in the state of Hawaii, and for my author photo for this book. I am profoundly grateful to my sons for their love and unconditional support.

Special thanks to my publisher-book designer and new friend, Susan Shankin, for believing in my book and forging ahead with a creative plan to design the concepts of the cover and the interior contents. She suggested meaningful changes to the cover and the manuscript, while supporting ideas and perspectives that I hold sacred. Her passion for excellence seamlessly linked and guided every step in the process. The staff of Precocity Press—Brenda Lange and Darcy Hughes—deserve a round of applause for their creative feedback, for guiding me to shape and perfect the manuscript, and for bringing it successfully to publication. To my sons and Precocity Press, I am forever grateful.

About the Author

Dr. Theresa (Tes) del Tufo's love of learning and books, and her partnership with Delaware libraries, inspired her to become an author, and share her experience and knowledge. In her newest book, *Women Powered! A New Paradigm of Influence and Equity* (McFarland Publishers, 2021), she offers women a guideline for action on how to gain and keep power. She proposes the systematic application of a NEW power construct—*Character-Driven Leadership* (originally called WomenPower Paradigm), which involves the development of key character traits and core competencies. Her recent book, *Behind the Golden Door: The Resilience of Today's Immigrants,* (Motivational Press, 2017) chronicles the real-life struggles and triumphs of immigrants to this country. *The Fullness of Nothing: Discover the Hidden Joy that Surrounds You* (Motivational Press, 2015), profiles the lives of people with disabilities who have managed to lead successful and happy lives despite the daily challenges confronting them. She is the author *SoloPower: How to Harness the Secret Energy of Living Alone* (Motivational Press, 2014) that explores the happiness, challenges, and transition stages of solo living. She is also the co-author of a technical publication on organizational excellence, *The Measure of Library Excellence: Linking the Malcolm Baldrige Criteria and the Balanced Scorecard to Assess Service Quality* (McFarland Publishers, 2008).

Tes is a first-generation immigrant from the Philippines. As a child, she survived the ravages of war during the Japanese occupation of the country. Her family had to escape to the mountains since her father was wanted for publishing anti-Japanese propaganda. As a young bride and immigrant, she had no family to support her after the untimely death of her husband. As a single parent, she raised two young sons and put them through college, while working on her doctoral degree and holding a full-time job.

In March of 2009, Tes was inducted into the *Delaware Women's Hall of Fame* by Governor Jack Markell. The award is the most prestigious recognition bestowed on Delaware women for lifetime achievement and outstanding accomplishments. She is the recipient of many other awards, including an Outstanding Service Award from the Developmental Disability Council and the Women's Vocational Services. She was also recognized in 2009 and 2012 as one of the Top 100 Business Entrepreneurs in Delaware, Virginia, Maryland, and the District of Columbia.

www.ingramcontent.com/pod-product-compliance
Lightning Source LLC
LaVergne TN
LVHW090514110826
845146LV00003B/856

* 9 7 9 8 9 9 0 9 4 6 0 8 8 *